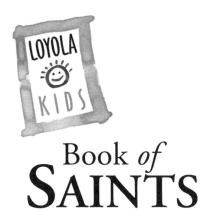

Book *of* SAINTS

LOYOLA KIDS
Book *of* SAINTS

Amy Welborn

illustrated by

Ansgar Holmberg, C.S.J.

LOYOLAPRESS.

CHICAGO

LOYOLAPRESS.
3441 N. ASHLAND AVENUE
CHICAGO, ILLINOIS 60657

Cover and interior design by Vita Jay
Cover and interior art by Ansgar Holmberg, C.S.J.

Library of Congress Cataloging-in-Publication Data
Welborn, Amy.
   The Loyola kids book of saints /Amy Welborn.
      p. cm.
   Summary: Explains what saints are and introduces the morals and values of various saints.
   ISBN-13: 978-0-8294-1534-6
   ISBN-10: 0-8294-1534-3
    1. Christian saints—Biography—Juvenile literature. [1. Saints.] I. Title.

BX4658 .W45 2001
282' .092'2—dc21
[B]   2001029894

Printed in the United States of America
08 09 10 11 12 Bang 14 13 12 11 10

 CONTENTS

What is a saint?

Do you have any heroes?

I bet you do. Think for just a minute about the people you think are great. Think about people you want to be like when you grow up.

Who are they? Your parents? Your grandparents? A teacher? An athlete, a singer, or a world leader?

Most of us have heroes. Heroes help us figure out what's important in life and what it takes to be the kind of person we want to be.

Did you know that the church has heroes too? They're called saints.

You've heard of saints. There's a good chance you go to a parish or a school named after one. Maybe your town even bears the name of a saint—such as San Francisco or St. Louis. Perhaps you have something else in common with a saint: your very own name.

Reminders of saints are all around us. But did you ever wonder what exactly a saint is? Did you ever stop to wonder how the saint you're named after got to be a saint in the first place? Let's see if we can find answers to these big questions.

SAINTS ARE HOLY PEOPLE

When you think about the saints you've heard of, such as the Blessed Virgin Mary, St. Francis, or St. Thérèse, probably the first word that comes to your mind is *holy*. But what does that mean? What is a holy person?

What is a saint?

It's a simple answer, really. Holy people put God and his will first. Nothing else in the lives of holy people can even come close to competing with God—not money, not possessions, not fame, not even physical comfort.

Holy people listen to God and let him work through them. They try to see people as God sees them. They also try to treat them as he would. That's why most saints are known for, among other things, the way they helped the poor, the sick, and the outcast. Hardly anyone else in the world pays attention to such people, but God never forgets them, so the saints don't either!

All saints are holy people, but that doesn't mean they're all exactly alike. In this book, you'll find young saints and old saints. Saints are men and women, boys and girls. They come from all over the world, and they have many different skin colors. They all have different talents too. No two saints are alike. Each holy man or woman shares different gifts with the world, building up God's kingdom in his or her own unique way.

SAINTS ARE MODELS FOR US

Sometimes when we listen to Jesus' words, they seem so very hard to follow. Sometimes we wish that God were easier to understand.

Saints—those joyful, holy people—show us that Jesus' words aren't impossible to live by. They show us that no matter who we are or what our talents may be, it's possible for us to put Jesus first. And putting Jesus first will bring us more happiness than we could ever imagine.

Saints also show us that God is real and that the strength and grace he gives us is real too. Saints were able to do amazingly brave things not because they were so strong themselves, but because God made them strong. Saints show us what a difference God's love can make in the lives of people who suffer. Saints wrote letters, books, and prayers to share with us their deepest moments with God.

So when we wonder where God is, saints are there to show us. When we wonder if following God is really possible, saints are there to show us that it is.

SAINTS PRAY FOR US IN HEAVEN

Have you ever asked someone to pray for you? Have you ever prayed for someone else?

I'm sure you have. Praying for someone is a way of loving that person. It's a way to show compassion and care. It's a way to try to help.

Now, you already know that saints are holy people who put God first. That means that they put love first, since God is love. Saints never stop loving and never stop caring. They don't stop loving even after they've died!

Death is not the end of life. Jesus brings us eternal life with him. The saints, holy people that they are, continue to love as they enjoy life in heaven with God.

Think of it this way: You ask your friends to pray for you or for other people all the time. Well, up in heaven, you've got a whole bunch of very special friends—the saints! That's why we talk to saints now, even after they've passed away. We know that they're with God. We know that they are filled with love. And just like our friends on earth, they're happy to pray for us all the time and any time we ask them to!

SAINTS ARE HONORED BY THE CHURCH

Millions of holy men and women have walked on God's earth. You probably know some yourself.

Sometimes holy people are so special and so close to God that the church decides to recognize them. These are the people we call "saint" with a capital *S*. These are people the church wants the whole world to know about. That way the whole world can see how much goodness and joy God's love can bring into a person's life.

The church recognizes these very special holy people by canonizing them. *Canonizing* means declaring that a person was a special friend of God and because of that is a special friend of everyone in the world.

This is how canonization usually starts. After a holy person dies, people start to talk about his or her God-centered life. A few people may start to honor the holy person by asking that person to pray for them. People honor a holy person by asking him or her to pray for their specific problems. If those prayers are answered, the word spreads. Eventually, if enough people are convinced that the holy person is special enough for the whole world to know about, they ask the church to decide whether the holy person should be declared a saint with a capital *S*.

It takes a long time to make a decision like that. At the Vatican, the center of the Catholic Church, the officials in charge must know everything about the holy person's life. They must read everything the person wrote. They must listen to and carefully examine stories of answered prayers and even of miracles that are related to that holy person.

If they decide that knowing about the holy person would help the people of the world grow in God's love, they give the holy person the title of "Venerable." If, after that, more people do grow in faith and have their prayers answered, the holy person is declared "Blessed." At that time, the church appoints a certain day in the year to be the holy person's feast day.

And finally, after a number of years, the Vatican officials may declare this holy person a "Saint." They make this decision after many people have come to understand God more and have had more strength to follow Jesus and to pray—all because of knowing about the holy person's life.

So a saint is a person who puts God first, lets Jesus live through him or her, is a model for us, prays for us in heaven, and is honored by the whole church for all that he or she has done to bring God's love into the world.

In this book, you'll read about lots of saints from all over the world and from all across time. You'll see that holiness doesn't have any boundaries. Any person of any age, living anywhere at any time, can put Jesus first and let God strengthen him or her to do marvelous things.

Even you!

PART 1

SAINTS ARE

People Who Love Children

*Let the children come to me, and do
not prevent them; for the kingdom of
heaven belongs to such as these.*

Matthew 19:14

St. Nicholas *4th century*

December 6

Children all over the world know him and love him.

In Germany, he's Kriss Kringle. In France, he's Pere Noel. British children call him Father Christmas. Of course, you know him as Santa Claus.

He's got another name, you know. It's an ancient one that goes back hundreds of years. It's one of the very first names people called him: St. Nicholas.

Children tell lots of fun stories about Santa Claus, Pere Noel, or Kriss Kringle. All of these stories remind us of how much we're loved and of how happy we are when we give. The earliest stories we know were told about St. Nicholas, the bishop of Myra.

Hundreds of years ago, Nicholas lived in a seaside town named Myra, which is in the country we now call Turkey. Ever since he was a small child, Nicholas loved God more than anything. He studied hard, prayed often, and followed Jesus by helping the poor.

The people of Myra loved Nicholas so much that when their old bishop died, they immediately elected Nicholas to replace him. He served them well for a long time.

Nicholas was loved for one reason. He loved. He loved God and God's people so much that he would do anything for them.

Here is a story about Nicholas that has been passed down through many generations.

There was a man living in Myra who was very poor. This man had no wife, but he had three grown daughters who lived with him.

In those days, when a young woman got married, she had to bring money or property with her into the marriage. This is called a dowry. If a woman didn't have a dowry, she would never marry.

This man was so poor that he had no money for his daughters' dowries. And he didn't have enough money to support them either. He had, he believed, only one choice: to sell his daughters into slavery. Nicholas heard about this terrible situation. Late one night, Nicholas crept to the man's home and threw something through the window. It was a bag of gold—enough to pay the dowry for his oldest daughter.

The man was overjoyed, and his daughter was too. She married, but her father was still left with a problem. Two, to be exact. What about the two younger daughters? Sadly, he prepared to send them away.

Nicholas returned one night and again threw a bag of gold through the window. The father rejoiced. But he wondered who was helping him and why.

Of course, Nicholas didn't want the man to know. He knew that it's best to help others without letting them know we're helping them. If we help others in this way, we help because we truly want to and not because people will praise us for it.

But the father was determined. He had one daughter left and no money for a dowry. He certainly hoped he would be helped again, especially because he wanted to find out who was doing it. So he locked the windows and watched out the door.

Nicholas still wanted to help, but he didn't want to be seen. So, in the back of the house, far from the father's sight, he dropped the bag of gold for the third daughter right down the chimney!

Other stories are told about Nicholas. It's said that God worked through Nicholas's prayers to raise children from the dead—some who had been killed in a fire and another child who had drowned. All of these stories tell us the same thing about St. Nicholas. He lived for God, which means that he lived for love. If people were in need and he was able to help, St. Nicholas gave them hope and strength. St. Nicholas never paused for a minute to wonder what he should receive in return for his help. He only thought about what he could give to those who needed him.

Stories about St. Nicholas spread from his home in Turkey up to Russia, where he is still a very popular saint. Through the centuries, people passed on stories of him across the most northern parts of Europe, then to Germany, France, and England, and finally to the United States. The children in every country gave St. Nicholas a name in their own language, and ours is Santa Claus.

Christmas is a fun, exciting time, isn't it? It's fun because of all the time we get to spend with our families. It's fun because we do a lot of celebrating. It's fun because we get to think, sing, and pray about Jesus, who was born into the world to save us.

Christmas is also fun because we get to give. We can show our family and friends how much we love them by giving them special gifts that we make or buy.

We give because we're thankful. We're thankful for friendship and love and for all the people who take care of us. We're thankful to God for giving us life.

St. Nicholas was thankful too, and that's why at Christmastime we try to be just like him. He was so grateful for the life God had given him that he just couldn't stop giving joy and hope to others— no matter how far he had to travel or how many roofs he had to climb!

St. Nicholas showed his gratitude for God's gifts by giving to others. What gifts can your family share with those in need?

St. John Bosco *1815–1888*

January 31

Who's your favorite teacher?

If you're like most children, your favorite teacher is someone who cared a lot about you. That teacher cares enough to give you extra help when you needed it. Maybe she noticed when you were sad and cared enough to ask you why. Or maybe he worked really hard and did a good job, all because he cared about you.

Children throughout history have loved teachers who cared about them. In Italy, more than a hundred years ago, one special teacher was loved by the thousands of students he taught and helped during his lifetime. That teacher's name was Don John Bosco.

John Bosco grew up on a farm in Italy. When he was just nine years old, he had a very strange dream. He was in a field, surrounded by crowds of other boys who were all behaving very badly. Suddenly, the figure of a man appeared, glowing with light, and told little John that he was to be the leader of these children. Can you imagine how John felt? Of course he was surprised and afraid. He told the man he didn't see how he could help all those boys.

The figure, still shining with a peaceful, clear light, told John something very important. He said, "Not with blows will you help these boys, but with goodness and kindness." After he said this, the boys in John's dream stopped misbehaving, and they became calm.

From that point on, John knew what he wanted to do. He wanted to help boys who were troubled. And he wanted to help them with love, not with harshness or cruelty.

John Bosco's dream came true, but it took quite a long time. He had to study for years before he could be ordained as a priest. Then John Bosco had to find a way to help boys. He had to do all of this on his own. No one else was helping boys the way John's dream had told him to do it—with gentleness and kindness.

After he became a priest, John lived in Turin, a large city in northern Italy. At that time— the middle of the nineteenth century— Turin was a beautiful place to live for some people, but a terrible place for many others. New factories were being built all the time, and poor families were moving to Turin from the countryside, hoping they could get better jobs.

Sometimes they could get better jobs, but many times the factory jobs were worse than work on the farms. Factory workers made little money and had to live in dirty, crowded slums. Young Don Bosco (in Italy they call priests "Don" the same way we call them "Father") walked these streets with great sadness, seeing how hard life was for so many people. It was especially hard for young boys, who had no schools to help them. The boys were running wild, just like the boys in Don Bosco's dream.

One day, John was in the back of his church after Mass. He heard one of the church workers yelling, and he went to see what was wrong. The man was shouting at a boy who had come into the church on this chilly day to try to get warm. Don Bosco had never seen the boy before, but he told the man to stop yelling. The man wanted to know why.

"Because," said Don Bosco, "he's my friend."

From that moment, Don Bosco decided that the best way to help the poor boys of Turin was to be their friend. He invited the boy who'd come into the church to return the next week and bring some other boys with him. They came, and the next week they returned with even more boys. Soon Don Bosco had more than four hundred boys joining him on Sundays in the slums of the city.

Since Don Bosco didn't have a building to use at first, he had to do his work outside. It was a good thing anyway, because Don Bosco's work with these boys was really play. He took them on long walks into the country, where they had picnics and played games. He taught them about how much God loved them and how important it was for them to put God's love first in their lives. Every Sunday, he said Mass for the boys in whatever church he could find.

Don Bosco called his meeting with the boys an "oratory." *Ora* means "prayer" in the Latin language, and Don Bosco wanted his boys to understand that prayer is always the center of a happy life. With the help of many people, Don Bosco's oratory grew, first into a real school and then into an orphanage as well. The oratory's very first building was just a small shed, but by the end of Don Bosco's life, the oratory had grown to include a large group of buildings where hundreds of boys could live, learn, and play.

Don Bosco's students always remembered him with love because he loved them very much. In those days, most schools allowed teachers to punish students by hitting them, but Don Bosco wouldn't allow it. He wanted his teachers to always treat their students with respect and kindness. He wanted the teachers to be a part of their students' lives, not only by teaching them but also by joining in their games and listening to their problems.

When Don Bosco died in 1888, he left behind many schools and a religious order called the Salesians, named after another great saint, St. Francis de Sales. This order was devoted to passing on his message of love to boys and girls all over the world.

He also left behind thousands of students, young and old, who remembered the kind, gentle, and patient Don Bosco as the best teacher they'd ever had.

St. John Bosco knew that the best teaching is based on love. Why do you think that's true?

St. Elizabeth Ann Seton *1774–1821*

January 4

Saints love children.

They love poor children. They love sick children. They love the children they teach in school, and they love children who have lost their parents. They love children in every land all over the world.

And of course, saints love their very own children!

St. Elizabeth Ann Seton was the first person born in the United States to be canonized a saint. She did a lot of different things. She was a writer. She was a teacher. She was a leader.

Elizabeth Ann Seton was also the busy, loving mother to five children!

Elizabeth was born in New York and grew up during the American Revolution. Her father was a doctor, and her mother died when little Elizabeth was only three years old.

When she grew up, Elizabeth was known throughout New York City as a beautiful, generous, kind young woman. She was a Christian and was quite interested in religion, but she was not a Catholic. She was very popular—she went to lots of parties. And when she was twenty years old, she married William Seton, a successful businessman.

Elizabeth and William were happy together, and they were even happier when their babies were born. After nine years, they were the parents of three girls and two boys.

But life never follows a straight road, does it? Life hides sadness around corners and hardship on the other side of joy.

That's what Elizabeth discovered. Within a few years, her father died, her husband's father died, and the family business started to fail. To make matters worse, William himself fell ill.

Elizabeth and William decided that a trip might just help them come up with some answers to their problems. Italy was where they wanted to go. They thought the weather would help William, and they had friends in Italy who could help with their business.

So William, Elizabeth, and one of their children, eight-year-old Anna Maria, set off. They were excited and happy about this wonderful trip, and everything went very well—there were no terrible storms, no shipwrecks, and no pirates.

But at the end of their journey across the sea, the strangest thing happened. When their ship arrived in Italy, the officials on shore learned that a disease called yellow fever had broken out in New York. No one on the ship had yellow fever, but they had no proof that they were well.

Without that proof, the officials wouldn't allow the people to come into Italy. Everyone on board had to be kept in quarantine. That means that they weren't allowed contact with any people on land. They had to stay isolated until everyone was sure that the yellow fever had not been brought to Italy.

So William, Elizabeth, and Anna Maria were taken to a stone tower that stood in the middle of the bay outside the city. It was a place that had been used in the past to house lepers, but now it was to be their home for the next thirty days.

Elizabeth tried hard to keep everyone's spirits strong, but there was little she could do about her husband's health. Already ill, he only got worse in that cold, damp tower. The family was released from quarantine on December 19, but it was too late for William to get help. He died two days after Christmas.

Poor Elizabeth! There she was, in a foreign country with her daughter, while her four other children and a failed business were at home across the ocean.

What could she do? How would she and her children live?

Elizabeth Ann Seton had always been close to God, even as a child. As she grew older, every stage in her life—her happy marriage, the birth of each of her wonderful children—brought her even closer to God.

But all along, something had been missing. Once she was in Italy with her Catholic friends, Elizabeth discovered what it was. It was the peace of the Catholic faith, especially the loving presence of Jesus in the Eucharist.

When Elizabeth returned to New York, she thought long and hard. For months she prayed, reflected, and wrote in her journal. What should she do?

The answer was soon clear. Elizabeth had found the truth in the Catholic faith, so she would devote her life to it. On March 14, 1805, Elizabeth Ann Seton became a Catholic.

Once again, her life changed. You see, in those days, not many Catholics lived in the United States, and those who did faced a great deal of prejudice. None of Elizabeth's relatives understood what she was doing. And soon it became clear that the wealthy people of New York, people who'd been her friends since she was a child, were turning their backs on her.

Except for the peace that Elizabeth, and now her children, found in the Catholic faith, everything seemed to be getting worse by the day. She had no money. Her friends and even her family were treating her as if she had committed a crime, just because she had become a Catholic. Elizabeth tried to open a school in New York City, but her own children were the only pupils. Other people were afraid she'd try to make their children Catholic too!

One day, Elizabeth was sitting in the back of church, quietly praying. The priest had noticed her during Mass. Now he couldn't help noticing her again. Elizabeth's prayer seemed so deep and true that the priest couldn't help but wonder who she was. So he asked.

Elizabeth told him her name and her whole difficult story. The priest thought about it and decided that God had brought Elizabeth to this place. The priest needed help—he wanted to start a school back in his home state of Maryland. Perhaps Elizabeth was the one who could help. Would she be interested?

Of course she would. It was exactly what she had hoped for. Elizabeth's sons had already been sent to boarding school in Washington, but her three daughters were still with her. Together they moved to Maryland, first to the city of Baltimore, then to the country.

And there, Elizabeth started her school. She taught her own girls, as well as girls from all around the area, including African American and Native American girls. The first winter in the country was very hard—Elizabeth and her daughters lived in a log cabin with hardly anything on the windows and doors. It was cold, and sometimes they awakened to find that snow had blown in and covered the floors!

But Elizabeth's school grew. Other women came to join her as teachers. Soon it was decided that the women should be organized into an order of sisters, a group of women who give their lives to God in a special way, vowing to live for him alone.

Elizabeth agreed, but on a few conditions. She wanted her children to able to stay and keep living with her, and she wanted to always be free to tend to their needs. It was agreed, and the Sisters of Charity was born.

St. Elizabeth Ann Seton

Elizabeth Ann Seton loved children—all children. She bravely took care of her own children when she was all alone and friendless in New York. She taught them, cared for them, and most important, guided them into faith in Jesus. One of her daughters also became a sister, and one of her sons became an archbishop!

Through her work in the countryside of Maryland—building a school, helping it grow, and even writing textbooks and teaching—St. Elizabeth Ann Seton showed us that saints are people who really listen when Jesus says, "Let the little children come to me."

St. Elizabeth Ann Seton always tried to see the good that God wanted to come out of everything that happened to her, even the sad things. What lessons have hard times in your life taught you?

Blessed Gianna Beretta Molla *1922–1962*

April 28

How do you know if someone loves you?

Do they give you presents? Do they make you laugh? Are they nice to you? Do they let you do anything you want to do?

Sometimes we think those things are signs of love. We get angry with our parents when they're strict. We get upset when they ask us to do things that aren't fun—like homework or jobs around the house. We think they don't love us.

We're wrong. People who don't care about us at all can give us presents or make us laugh. Love is something else.

Love is really caring about another person and wanting the best for him or her. When we love someone, we act in his or her best interest, no matter how hard it might be for either of us.

But how do we know that that's what love is?

We know it because it's the way Jesus loved and lived. We know it because God *is* love.

Holy people are people who show us very clearly what love is, because they love just as Jesus did. They love everyone they meet, and they love the poor and the unwanted. They love the whole world, and they start with their own families.

In Italy not too long ago, a mother loved her children with Jesus' kind of love. Her name was Gianna Beretta Molla.

Gianna came from a large, happy family. Her parents taught her to love God and to serve God with whatever talents God had given her. Early on, Gianna decided that she wanted to serve God and God's people as a doctor.

So Gianna went to medical school. After she graduated, she set up a practice with her brother. They began treating the sick, especially children and poor people.

After many years of happily practicing medicine, Gianna married a man named Pietro, and they started having children. The babies came very quickly—first a boy, then a girl, then another girl. Gianna—mother, doctor, and wife—was very happy.

In 1961, Gianna found out that she was going to have another baby. She and her husband were overjoyed. But soon, bad news arrived. Gianna was sick.

A doctor told her that she had a tumor inside her, very close to where the baby was growing. The best way to save her own life would be to take much of the tumor out. But that meant that the baby would die.

Gianna said no. She told the doctors to take out as much of the tumor as they could without harming the baby. After the baby was born, she would try to get better on her own, but for now, the baby came first.

The doctors performed the surgery. As the months went on, Gianna and Pietro prayed. They prayed for their baby's safety, and they prayed for strength. Gianna was grateful to God for having given her a baby. She was willing to sacrifice whatever was necessary, even her own health, to help her baby.

In April, on Holy Saturday (the day before Easter Sunday), Gianna's baby was born. It was a girl, and they named her Emanuela, which means "God is with us."

But the doctors had sad news for Gianna. They had discovered that she was very, very sick. For seven days they worked to save her. They gave her the best medicines and their best care. Gianna only got worse.

That whole long week, Gianna continued to pray. She prayed for her children and her husband. She thanked God for giving her baby life.

Near the end of the week, it was clear that Gianna was not going to live. The doctors permitted her to leave the hospital. She was taken to her own home, to her own bed, and there she died.

Gianna Beretta Molla died in peace. Before she died, she told her husband that she had seen what awaited her in heaven, and she was not afraid. Her heart was full, even though she was suffering, because she was suffering for the sake of love.

Blessed Gianna loved the children she helped as a doctor, and she loved her own precious little ones. Her love was special because it was so much like the love that Jesus has for all of us. It was a love that was fearless and unafraid. It was a love that was totally unselfish. Like Jesus, Blessed Gianna Beretta Molla was willing to give anything for the sake of love—even her own life.

As Blessed Gianna shows us, sometimes love requires great sacrifice. Can you think of people in your life who have sacrificed for your sake?

 # PART 2

SAINTS ARE

People Who Love Their Families

Honor your father and your mother.

Exodus 20:12

St. Monica *332–387*

August 27

Moms are great, aren't they?

Moms are great when they fix our dinner, help us with our homework, and play games with us. Moms are great when they listen to our problems and take us to soccer practice. Moms are great when they worry.

Wait a minute. Did I really just say that moms are great when they worry?

If your mom has ever worried about you, you might not agree. You probably want her to trust you and to believe that you know what you're doing. You probably wish your mom wouldn't remind you to be safe every time you walk out the door or get on a bike.

A boy named Augustine who lived more than sixteen centuries ago had a mom just like yours. Her name was Monica. She loved Augustine a lot, and he loved her too.

Just like your mom, Monica loved her child so much that she had to worry about him. And just like you, Augustine was happy that his mom loved him, but her worrying bugged him. It took a long time for Augustine to really see that his mom worried for a good reason. She loved him and wanted him to be truly happy.

Monica, Augustine, and the rest of their family lived in North Africa during the fourth century. At that time, northern Africa was part of the Roman Empire. Many of the people who lived there were Christians, including Monica.

Little Augustine wasn't baptized, though. In the church in those days, baptism was still mostly for grown-ups. But like any good Christian parent, Monica worked hard to teach her son all about Jesus so that he would make the right decision later.

Augustine was a very smart boy. He went to school to learn how to be a teacher and a lawyer. Monica was excited. She knew that Augustine had a bright future ahead of him, maybe even as an important person in the Roman government.

Monica was happy about Augustine's career, but something even more important made her sad. When he grew up, Augustine didn't get baptized after all. He joined a religious group called the Manicheans. These people believed some strange and even dangerous things. They believed that there were two gods, a good one and an evil one. They believed that if you really wanted to be good, you shouldn't get married or have children.

When Augustine joined this strange group, Monica was angrier than she'd ever been with him. She was so angry that she told him something your mom probably has never told you—she told him he could never come back home.

But soon after that, Monica had a dream. In this dream, she saw something that made her feel much better—she and Augustine were standing next to each other.

She told her son about this. Augustine decided that it meant that one day his mother would join the Manicheans too, but Monica knew better! She knew God was telling her through her dream that someday Augustine would share her faith in Jesus. After that, even though Monica disagreed with Augustine's beliefs, she let him come back home.

Then Augustine decided to move far away—to Rome, across the sea from northern Africa. Monica didn't want him to go. She was afraid that if Augustine went so far away from home, he would never return to God.

Augustine went to the port. Of course, Monica went too, because she was still trying to talk Augustine out of leaving. On this calm, warm night, Augustine told her he had to wait for a better wind before he could set sail. But Augustine wasn't telling the truth. That very night, while Monica was sleeping, he caught another boat to Rome!

Many years later, Augustine wrote about this secret journey. He was really sorry he had lied to his mother, and he knew it was wrong. But he also knew that this step in his life had been the start of something wonderful. While crossing the ocean, he had come closer to Christ.

You can read about what happened to Augustine and exactly how he became a Christian in another part of this book (page 173). For now, we'll just talk about Monica and what she did to help.

That's right—a mother's work is never done, and that's the way it was for Monica. She had taught Augustine about Jesus when he was little and had prayed for him his whole life. All of those prayers were finally answered when Augustine was thirty-four years old and living in a city in Italy called Milan. He was almost ready to believe in Jesus, but first he needed answers to some hard questions.

You won't be surprised to know that by this time, Monica had moved to Milan too. She knew the bishop, Ambrose (you can read about him on page 197), and she knew that Ambrose was smart enough to answer her son's questions. She asked Ambrose to talk to Augustine. He did, and his answers helped Augustine finally open his heart to God.

Monica was overjoyed. But she did not live very long after that. She never saw Augustine become a priest and then a bishop. She never saw him lead the church through hard times and write important books that we still read today. But she knew that her son had come to God. Monica didn't have to worry anymore.

Although Monica's worrying had sometimes bothered Augustine, when he looked back on his life, he was always grateful.

His mother's prayers were an important reason why Augustine finally found happiness in God. He knew Monica had worried only because she loved him and wanted the best for him.

And that's why your mom worries too!

St. Monica prayed and hoped that her son Augustine would see how much God loved him. Do you have the same hopes for people in your family?

St. Cyril and St. Methodius *d. 869 and 885*

February 14

Brothers and sisters can get in the way sometimes.

Little sisters barge into your room and interrupt you when you're talking on the phone. Big brothers make fun of you and boss you around. And whether they're younger or older, brothers and sisters always seem to be ready for a fight or ready to let you take the blame for things you didn't do.

All of that may be true, but you have to admit that it's not true every minute.

Sometimes brothers and sisters can really help you out. Older brothers and sisters can help you learn how to ride your bike by yourself or do those hard math problems. Little brothers and sisters can be pretty cute and fun to play with, too.

And sometimes—every once in a while—you and your brothers or sisters manage to work together and accomplish something great.

Remember the snow fort? your mom's surprise birthday party? the time you cleaned the whole house together without being asked?

Brothers and sisters can sure be a pain sometimes. But it's also true that when you work together, good things happen.

Cyril and Methodius show us how brothers can work together to make the world a better place. They show us that having a brother or sister doesn't have to be such a pain.

These two brothers were born in Thessalonica, which is in the most northern part of Greece. Methodius was older. When he grew up, he held important government positions. Cyril was the more scholarly type. He studied philosophy and later taught it.

On the surface, Cyril and Methodius seem rather different, don't they? Methodius was involved in more practical, everyday matters, while Cyril seemed more interested in ideas.

But really, they had more in common than it seemed.

Both Cyril and Methodius put God first in their lives. Both of them were ordained priests and eventually joined monasteries. Methodius was the first to do this, leaving behind the world of government and laws. Cyril followed some time afterward, secretly. He'd become a very popular teacher, but he just wanted to get away and have lots of time to pray alone. After six months, though, Cyril was discovered. He was sent to another country where the people wanted to learn about Jesus.

The other important thing Cyril and Methodius had in common was that both brothers knew another language beside their own. They were Greek, but they were also familiar with the Slavonic language. This language was spoken in the area north of their own country, in much of what we now call Eastern Europe.

Their commitment to God and their knowledge of the Slavonic language would bring big changes to their lives. These were good changes too, and the brothers would go through them together.

Cyril and Methodius were asked to do a big job. The prince of the Slavic countries north of Greece had sent an urgent plea. His people very much wanted to know about Jesus. But of all the missionaries who had come to help, not one could speak their language. Not one could tell them about Jesus in words they really understood. Could anyone help?

Cyril and Methodius could. So together the brothers began their journey north.

The hardest thing about this job was the language. The problem wasn't speaking it—Cyril and Methodius could do that with ease. The problem was that the Slavonic people had no alphabet. They had no written language and no books. They spoke, taught their children how to speak, and passed stories down by word of mouth. But they never wrote anything down.

So of course, the first thing the brothers had to do was make it possible for the language to be written. Cyril invented an alphabet for the language, and that alphabet, which is still used in all the Slavic languages (including Russian) is named after him. It's called Cyrillic.

But that's not all. Once Cyril and Methodius arrived, they worked hard to do what all missionaries do. They taught people about Jesus and taught them how followers of Jesus treat each other.

Cyril and Methodius also translated the words of the Mass into the Slavonic language so the people could better understand what the Mass was all about and could worship God in words they knew. The brothers translated the Scriptures too so that the people could read stories about Jesus in their own language.

This job had a dangerous side. Leaders of neighboring lands didn't like the work of Cyril and Methodius. They believed that giving the Slavonic people their own language and the Christian faith would make them stronger and harder to control and conquer. Several times, Cyril and Methodius had to travel to Rome to defend and explain their work to the pope. Every time, the pope approved their work. After a while, as a sign of what he thought of their work, the pope ordained both of them bishops.

Cyril died shortly after being ordained a bishop, so Methodius had to continue the work alone for the last sixteen years of his life. You can be sure that he missed his brother very much.

So you see, that's the way it is with brothers and sisters.

You're different, but in many ways you're the same. With brothers and sisters, you have a choice. You can fight over your differences, or you can combine your different gifts and talents just as Cyril and Methodius did, using them to help spread the love of Jesus and make the world a better place!

Cyril and Methodius were brothers who worked together to spread the good news of Jesus. If you have brothers or sisters, think about the gifts and talents they have. How can all of you use those gifts and work together as a family to bring God's love to everyone you meet?

St. Thérèse of Lisieux *1873–1897*

October 1

Where did you first learn about God?

Did you first learn about God in religion class? in Sunday school? in church on Sunday morning?

If you're like most kids, the good news about God's love came to you long before you sat in a classroom or knelt in church. Most likely, you first heard about God from your family.

It was probably your mom, your dad, or one of your grandparents who taught you about God. They taught you your prayers. They read you Bible stories at bedtime. They answered all of those questions you had about the crucifix on the wall, the Advent candles, and no meat on Fridays during Lent.

You learned about God from your family in another way too.

What's the most important thing anyone can know about God? That he loves you, right? Well, where's the first place you were loved? And who are the first people who loved you?

That's right. You were first loved right in your own home, by the people in your own family.

So even as a tiny baby lying in a crib, you were learning about God. When people cuddled you and fed you, they were teaching you what love is. As you got older and your family listened to your problems and had fun with you, they were teaching you what love is.

They weren't teaching you with words. They were teaching you with their hearts and their actions. That way, when you got old enough to hear about God's love, you could recognize it!

A little more than a hundred years ago, a young girl lived in a very loving family. On the outside, there was nothing special about them. They weren't wealthy, and they weren't royalty. They were just a family. They were the Martins.

Mrs. Martin had had ten children, but many of them had died when they were just babies. By the time the youngest—Thérèse—was born, only four others were still alive. All of them were girls: Marie, Pauline, Celine, and Leonie.

The Martins had a happy home, and when little Thérèse was born, she was surrounded by love. Her parents loved God very much, and they put him at the center of their family's life, every hour of every day.

When Thérèse was four years old, something quite sad happened. Her mother died. Little Thérèse was terribly upset, and she never forgot how lost and confused she felt when her mother died.

But luckily for Thérèse, she had those four older sisters. All of them took care of their little sister. They did what their mother would have wanted. They taught Thérèse about God's love and showed her what love is. Her favorite sister was Pauline.

When Thérèse was about ten years old, Pauline became a nun. The convent she joined was very strict. Thérèse could go visit her sister, but she could only see her through a little window in a wall that was in the middle of the convent's parlor. The nuns, called Carmelites, were so strict because they wanted to spend their time focusing only on God.

But Pauline could write letters, and she did. She sent Thérèse a notebook that was decorated with beautifully drawn flowers. She told Thérèse to write in this book every day all the prayers and good deeds she did. Pauline told Thérèse that every prayer and every loving act was like a little flower. If Thérèse watered these little flowers with even more prayers and love, they would keep growing and growing, making the world a beautiful place for everyone. The book was very special to Thérèse.

In just a few years, her sister Marie joined the convent too. Thérèse was praying more and more, getting closer and closer to Jesus. When she was only fourteen, she decided it was time for her to follow her sisters and give her life to Jesus.

It wasn't easy. Her choice made her father sad at first, but soon he agreed. Unfortunately, the bishop didn't agree. Because Thérèse was so young, the bishop didn't want to give her permission to start such a hard life.

But Thérèse knew what she wanted. And she knew someone who could change the bishop's mind: the pope!

Thérèse and her father traveled to Rome. No one knew what Thérèse was going to do when she entered St. Peter's Basilica with hundreds of other people to see the pope. No one knew that this young girl, so strong and so full of love for Jesus, could be so brave.

Thérèse went right up to Pope Leo, knelt in front of him, and blurted out her story. She told him that even though she was young, she wanted to enter the convent. Would he please give her his permission?

He didn't exactly. He told Thérèse that if it was God's will, she would be able to enter. A few months later, right after Christmas, the letter came. The bishop had given her permission to enter the convent! It was the best Christmas present Thérèse had ever received.

For the next ten years, Thérèse lived a quiet life in the convent. She prayed, worked hard with the other sisters—including her real ones—and studied God's word.

Thérèse had one goal in life: to love God. She knew that God had given her the gift of life. She knew that God had saved her through Jesus' suffering and resurrection from the dead. What else was there to do but use every minute of her day to thank him?

So Thérèse loved God. With every sweep of the floor or stir of the kitchen pot, she loved God. With every friendly nod to even the most difficult nun in the convent, she loved God. With every step, Thérèse loved God.

And finally, Thérèse loved God with pain, sickness, and suffering.

She was so young when she died—only twenty-four years old. She had suffered terribly from tuberculosis, a disease that damages your lungs, makes it hard to breathe, and makes you cough up blood.

Even with all of that pain, Thérèse loved God and thanked him for life. She planted little flowers of love and care for everyone around her.

You won't believe how those flowers grew. Before she died, Thérèse wrote down all of her thoughts about loving God. She also wrote down stories about her life. After she died, all of these things were published in a book. Within just a few years, millions of people had read the book. They learned more about God's love from Thérèse's simple words than they ever could from fat, hard-to-read religion books.

Just think about it. Thérèse had been raised in love by her family and had lived her whole adult life in a convent. She quietly worked, prayed, and cared for others. She knew only a few people. She spent her days in the same simple rooms, eating the same simple food, and wearing the same simple clothes.

But today, millions of people know and love Thérèse. Her words are some of the wisest words ever written about God and his love.

Thérèse's life was full of flowers. They were little at first, just tiny seeds planted by her parents and sisters. Thérèse cared for the flowers. She watered them with the love she learned from her family, added her own love, and shared the flowers—with the people close to her and with the whole world. Her flowers grew into an abundant garden.

And what a lovely garden it is!

St. Thérèse learned about God's love from her family. How can the members of your family be strong signs of God's love to each other?

Blessed Frédéric Ozanam *1813–1853*

September 9

When we love God, we just can't keep it inside.

God's love flows out of us in every direction, touching every soul we meet, every minute of the day. When we love God, we're seeing the world through his eyes, not just through our own. And since God loves every person on earth and every part of creation, we're going to love all those people and all of creation too.

Look at it this way. You love your dad, right? Suppose your dad has a garden that's his pride and joy. Every day, Dad takes a few minutes to go work on his garden, pulling weeds and feeding his plants. It's something he's proud of, and it's something that gives him a lot of peace after a busy day.

Would you ever in a million years think about going out to that garden, ripping out the plants, and stomping them flat on the ground? If your dad had to go out of town and he left you in charge of the garden, would you ever even think of letting those plants die?

Of course not. You love your dad, and your dad loves the garden. You're going to care for the garden too.

Here's another example. You have a really good friend. She's your best friend, in fact, and you know that your friend really loves her mom.

Even if you're not crazy about your friend's mom, would you ever say mean things to her? Would you ever say mean things about her to your friend, even in secret?

You wouldn't do those things because that would be disrespectful. And you know that you should do your best to love every person your friend loves.

That's the way it is when we love God. He doesn't belong to us. He's the God of all people, everywhere. And he loves each person enough to come to earth, to live, to suffer, and to die for that person's sake.

If we love God, we cannot turn our back on even one of his beloved. It's that simple.

Blessed Frédéric Ozanam knew this truth, and he lived it out in an amazing way throughout his forty short years of life. Frédéric loved all the people he met in work and in school. He especially loved the poor. And of course, he loved his wife and his daughter too.

Frédéric Ozanam was a Frenchman with a brilliant mind and a big heart. He studied to be a lawyer but was interested in philosophy, religion, and literature as well. When he was a young man, he went to study in Paris, hoping to become a lawyer. This is what his father wished for him.

In those days, France was in great turmoil. The church was under attack from many places, especially from the government and the universities. Every day when Frédéric went to his classes, he had to listen to his professors mock his faith and declare that Christianity was a dead, useless religion.

These attacks didn't weaken Frédéric's faith. They made him want to study his faith more and see its truth more deeply. Soon Frédéric became known throughout the university as a smart, able defender of faith in Jesus.

Once, in the middle of a debate, amidst all the words and ideas, a challenge was tossed Frédéric's way.

"Let us be frank, Mr. Ozanam. Let us also be very particular. What do you do besides talk to prove the faith you claim is in you?"

This question hit Frédéric with great force. He was being asked, quite simply, "Sure, you say you believe. But what do you do to live your faith every day?"

(That's a good question for all of us, isn't it?)

Frédéric thought about his life. He wasn't a bad person. But the other speaker had a point. Frédéric said that he loved Jesus. Jesus often spoke of how important it was for those who say they love him to help the poor, the sick, and the outsiders.

If Frédéric really loved Jesus as he said he did, shouldn't he be loving the world the exact same way? Shouldn't he, as Jesus did, be giving his time and energy to bringing peace to those who were suffering?

Soon Frédéric had a chance to do just that. A terrible disease called cholera swept through Paris, killing more than a thousand people every day. As Frédéric walked to his classes with his friends, he could see the sick people's pain and misery, the orphaned children, and the hungry families.

But what could one person do?

Well, Frédéric decided that he could help one person in the morning and another person in the afternoon. If he had friends, together they could bring comfort to a few more. Why not?

So, along with six of his university friends, Frédéric started helping. The first day, they took the wood they had chopped for their own fire and gave it to a poor family. They went into the poorest neighborhoods, bringing food and medicine, clothing and shoes.

This little group grew quickly. France was experiencing great poverty at this time, and many people were anxious to help. Within a few years, thousands of people throughout France had joined Frédéric's group. By then, the group had grown into an organization called the Society of St. Vincent de Paul. (You can read about St. Vincent de Paul on page 255.)

Frédéric loved the poor. He helped thousands of them and wrote many articles defending their rights. But Frédéric also loved someone else. Two people, to be exact. Although most of his busy days were spent pouring out his love to the suffering, a little corner of his life was devoted to two special people: his wife, Amélie, and his daughter, Marie.

Frédéric had always known that marriage is a beautiful, holy union blessed by God, but before he'd met Amélie, he wasn't sure if he should marry or become a priest. As busy as he was, he was feeling a little lonely and sad. He didn't know which path—marriage or the priesthood—would bring him peace of mind.

In fact, it was a priest friend who helped Frédéric decide that he needed to marry. This friend knew just the right woman. Without Frédéric knowing why, the priest brought him to Amélie's family home, where she sat in a sunny corner of a room, playing with and caring for her sick brother. Almost at once, Frédéric fell in love.

They were married on the twenty-third of June. On the twenty-third day of every single month for the rest of their marriage, Frédéric gave Amélie a bouquet of flowers.

Frédéric Ozanam died when he was only forty years old. He left Amélie and his five-year-old daughter, Marie, behind to remember him and his love. But they weren't the only ones to remember, were they?

Frédéric loved with the heart of Jesus, and that kind of love is impossible to forget. The people of France, especially the poor of Paris, remembered Frédéric. The friends who had joined in his work remembered him. And even today, as the work of the St. Vincent de Paul Society continues around the world and maybe even in your very own parish, Frédéric Ozanam continues to touch the poor and the suffering with the love of Jesus.

Who can we see with the eyes of Jesus today? Will we meet someone today who needs the love of Jesus? What is our answer to the question Frédéric had to answer?

What will we do to live our faith today?

Blessed Frédéric Ozanam knew that his faith called him to action, not just words. How does your family live out Jesus' call to follow him?

PART 3

SAINTS ARE

People Who Surprise Others

For the foolishness of God is wiser than human wisdom, and the weakness of God is stronger than human strength.

1 Corinthians 1:25

St. Simeon Stylites *390–459*

January 5

"Are you even listening to me? Yes, you—I'm talking to you!"

Does this sound familiar? Does your mom sometimes have a hard time getting you to listen to her? Do your teachers?

Sometimes you really don't hear your mom. You run through the kitchen so fast that you kind of hear some words drifting around your head, but you don't quite catch them. It may have been something about the garbage or the dog, but you're not quite sure.

Or maybe you did hear, and you could even repeat the words that were spoken to you, but you didn't really *listen*.

Perhaps your teacher has told you a million times over the past two weeks that you really should study for the big vocabulary test and not wait until the night before. Every day, you should go over a few words so you won't have so much to learn at the very last minute.

And yet here you are, at the last minute, with so much left to learn and no time left to learn it.

You should have listened, right?

People speak to us all the time. They tell us some pretty important things too. But even if we hear them, we don't always listen. Sometimes people have to do strange things to get us to pay attention. Or they have to let us fail so we can figure out on our own that we should have listened.

What if someone talked to you from a seat on a pillar that rose sixty feet from the ground? Would that get your attention?

It's strange and it's surprising, but it could happen.

Simeon Stylites spent forty years in the desert, sitting on top of a pillar, praying, fasting, and talking to people about Jesus.

And people listened.

It's certainly an odd way to live and a pretty unusual way of trying to follow God. But it's exactly what Simeon felt called to do.

He wasn't the only one. During the same period of time, quite a few solitary hermits lived scattered throughout the deserts of Arabic lands. They lived on crusts of bread and little water. They wore few clothes or, at the very least, quite uncomfortable clothes. They spent their time in caves or on top of big pillars. *Stylite* comes from the Greek word for pillar: *stylos.*

Very early in his life, Simeon had decided that if he was going to be close to God, he needed to suffer physically. He knew that this wasn't what God wanted for everyone. But for him it was a way to teach himself that the needs of the body weren't important. By living simply and learning to endure pain, Simeon could train himself to depend on God alone for his happiness. He would no longer let his happiness depend on how full his stomach was or how warm he was at night.

Simeon tried many different ways of living before he settled on his pillar. He tried monasteries, but the way of life he wanted was too hard even for the monks who lived there. He tried to live in huts with no roofs or in caves, but even that was too easy.

The other problem was that even though he was trying to live this hard life in private, people were starting to seek him out for advice. All that suffering and prayer had made Simeon a very wise man indeed. Word of his wisdom got out, and people wouldn't leave him alone.

So Simeon decided to sit on a pillar. His first pillar extended about ten feet off the ground. He lived on that for about four years, then moved to a higher one. Eventually, he found the right height: about sixty feet off the ground! He lived there for the last sixteen years of his life.

Simeon didn't just perch up there, balanced on top of the pole. His home, day and night, was a small platform that was about twelve square feet. On top of that pillar, he prayed. He also fasted, eating nothing at all during Lent every year and not much more at other times.

As you can imagine, Simeon became almost a tourist attraction. Curious people came from far and wide to see the strange man on top of the pillar. When they arrived, they found a man who was wild looking and intense, but who spoke clearly and quite soundly about God's love.

People came to Simeon to ask him questions about life. People who were fighting came to have Simeon help them make peace. Emperors and bishops wrote to Simeon asking for his advice, and he sent it back to them in letters he dictated.

It was as if, high up on that pillar, Simeon was sitting in a special place between heaven and earth, and from there, he could be trusted to tell the truth about God.

Simeon lived in very rough times. People who lived in and roamed through the deserts were tough and hard. If they were going to hear about Jesus, they needed someone just as tough as they were to get them to listen. Simeon, who lived in the open, trusting completely in God to take care of him and give him peace, was just the person to get those tough desert wanderers to listen. Those who saw Simeon and wrote about him tell us that thousands of people did indeed become Christians because of him.

Simeon was certainly a surprising man. But he wasn't surprising because he wanted to get attention for himself. He was surprising because the people of his time needed a big surprise to get them to listen to the important message he had to share. Just like you need someone to do something strange to get you to listen.

We're surrounded by the truth. But the fact is that sometimes we don't listen at all—until someone uses a very odd, surprising way to tell it to us!

St. Simeon Stylites surprised others with the way he chose to follow Jesus. What are the surprising ways in which Jesus has spoken to you?

St. Celestine V *1215–1296*

May 19

Congratulations!

To be put in charge of the school newspaper is quite an honor. Of course you can handle it!

And how about you? You play piano really well. Why are you so shocked that the music teacher asked you to play with the choir at the Christmas concert?

No, we didn't forget about you either. You've always been so good with little kids. You won't mind helping the preschool teacher with her Sunday school class every week for the rest of the year, right?

Doesn't it feel great when other people recognize your talents? Isn't it flattering when people tell you that you are the right person for an important job?

Sometimes doing something new leads us to better things than we expected. That big step into more responsibility is just what we need to grow or to help others. That new job helps us realize how strong we can be if we put our fears aside.

But—gulp!—what if it just doesn't work out?

What if all the other kids working on the paper won't cooperate with you? What if those piano pieces are harder than you expected? What if the teacher you're supposed to help starts missing a lot of classes and you end up having to teach all those little kids by yourself?

What would you do?

When we make a promise, it's important to do all we can to keep it. But sometimes we get into a situation that's really too much for us. When that happens, we might hurt someone, even the person we're supposed to help.

This kind of thing happens more than you know. In fact, believe it or not, it even happened to the pope once!

Peter di Morone was a very holy man. Being holy means being close to God and living the way God is calling you to live. God calls people to be holy in many different ways. Some people find holiness in marriage and in having a family. Some people find holiness in doing their jobs well and in ways that help others.

Peter had a different way of being holy. He was a hermit.

Hermits are people who live by themselves, away from towns and cities and other people. Many great Christians were hermits. They believed that the best way for them to feel close to God was to spend as much time as they could praying by themselves.

That is what Peter did. He was a monk who lived in Italy during the thirteenth century. From the time he was twenty, he lived as a hermit. When he first decided to follow God this way, he lived on a mountain, in a hole so small that he could fit in it only by lying down.

Later, he moved to a cave. Peter spent his days and nights there, concentrating on the most important thing in life: God. To help himself focus only on God, he ate very little. He didn't eat any meat, and he fasted every day except Sunday. He slept on the cold ground, using a rock as a pillow. He wore a shirt made of rough horsehair and even wore a heavy chain around his waist.

It certainly seems like a strange way to live, but Peter did all of this because it helped him grow closer to God. He made himself uncomfortable so that he would learn to ignore what his body wanted and just focus on his soul.

I'm sure you know what happened next. After all, if you spent your days and nights thinking about math problems, what would happen to you? People would hear about how smart you were getting in math, and they'd come to you for help.

This is what happened to Peter. As the years went by, he grew closer and closer to God. People heard about the holy monk living in the hills, and they came to ask him how they could get closer to God. People all over Italy started talking about Peter. Surely he was the holiest man in the land!

Many miles away, the pope died. For two years, the cardinals tried to figure out who the new pope should be, but they could never settle on the right person. With no leader, the church started having problems. Peter heard about the problems and wrote the church officials a letter, telling them how concerned he was. The cardinals read the letter and had an idea.

Peter should be the pope!

As you can imagine, Peter didn't like this idea very much. He wanted to keep leading the simple life of a hermit. If he were pope, he would have to live in a palace with many other people. He would have to make decisions and meet with other people all day. Besides, Peter was seventy-nine years old!

But Peter decided that maybe this was God's will, so he accepted the position and took the name of Celestine V.

From the beginning, the new pope did things differently. He rode on a donkey to his crowning as pope. Instead of living in comfort, he built a little wooden room in the palace that would be his home. When he was elected, Christmas was on its way, so Peter wanted to prepare. He asked other people to meet and make decisions without him so that he could be alone and pray.

Peter didn't do this because he wanted to hurt anyone. He had been a hermit for more than fifty years. By living that way, he had helped many people, and in his heart he knew that a pope's way of serving God was different. Peter had gifts, but they weren't the kind of gifts that would help a pope do a good job.

So, four months after he was elected, Pope Celestine V did something no pope had ever done before (and no pope has done since). He resigned.

He asked for forgiveness for any trouble he'd caused, removed his elegant robes, and put on his rough hermit's clothes. He was no longer Pope Celestine V. Once again, he was Peter, the simple hermit, the person he knew God had called him to be all along.

Peter had to make a very hard decision. It can happen to any of us. But if you get in over your head, just remember this: If you take some time to pray and ask God to show you the best way to use your talents, God will help you. If you figure out that you're just not the person for the job, don't worry about what people will think of you. Don't worry about disappointing other people. They'll get over it, and God will take care of things.

And later on, when you find the job that's just right for your talents, you'll see for sure that it was all for the best!

St. Celestine had to make some hard choices about how to use his talents. Think about your gifts and talents. Are you using them in the best way you can right now?

St. Joan of Arc *1412–1431*

May 30

What's a surprise?

It's something we don't expect.

Think of times when you were surprised. Maybe you walked into the house and found a birthday party waiting for you. Maybe you were unpleasantly surprised by a bad grade on a paper you thought was pretty good.

Sometimes people surprise us when they turn out to be different than we thought they were. This can be either bad or good.

Maybe a person we thought was our friend shocks us by talking behind our back and making us feel left out. She's not the person we thought she was.

Or maybe that kid in the back of the class—the one we thought was a hopeless loser because of the way he looked and talked—turns out to be a fun kid. In fact, maybe he's the most interesting person we've met in a long time. He's not the person we thought he was.

That's the thing about people. They always surprise us.

That's why it's so dangerous to judge other people before we really get to know them. Our judgment puts them in little boxes, and then we can't see them for who they really are.

St. Joan of Arc was one of the most surprising people who ever lived. She was just a peasant girl who should have never made it into even one paragraph of a history book. But she burst through the walls of that box, and because of her, an entire country was rescued.

Joan of Arc's life took that surprising turn for one reason. She followed her conscience.

Joan's parents were poor farmers who lived in the French countryside. She was one of five children, and like her brothers and sisters, she spent her childhood learning lots of different skills. Joan learned how to farm and garden and how to care for sheep and pigs. She also learned how to spin wool into yarn and to weave.

The young French girl's life was no different from anyone else's— until she was about fourteen years old. It was then that something distracted Joan's attention from the animals, the farm, and the garden. Deep inside her heart, voices spoke to her conscience. These voices gave her important things to think about.

Joan came to understand that the voices were from three saints: St. Michael the Archangel, St. Catherine of Alexandria, and St. Margaret. For two years, Joan listened to the voices. She told no one about them. She just kept listening, trying to understand.

At the time, England and France were fighting a long, terrible war. The English forces controlled much of France, and the true king of France was unable to take his throne.

After listening to her conscience for two years, Joan realized that it would be her job to drive the English army from France and save her country. And because she knew that the voices in her heart were from heaven, she knew that she would succeed.

Now stop and think about this for a moment.

A sixteen-year-old peasant girl, poor and uneducated, realizes that she is being called to free her country. *She* is being called—not strong soldiers, not educated politicians, not wealthy princes.

Are you surprised? Just imagine how surprised Joan was!

But you know what it's like when you know that something's right. If you don't follow your heart and your conscience, you'll never rest. It will bother you forever, nagging you and making you wonder.

So off Joan went. The first person she found was a commander of the French army. He just laughed at her and said that she should be sent back to her father to be punished.

But Joan went back to that commander and told him that the French had suffered a terrible defeat outside a city called Orleans. Again, he laughed. But days later, he received news of the defeat. Then the commander began to take Joan seriously. Perhaps her wisdom and insight were coming from God after all.

So the commander gave Joan permission to meet the king. Even that would not be simple. The king's staff brought Joan into a huge crowd in which the king, dressed in ordinary clothes, was hidden. They wanted to test Joan, to see if she really had special knowledge from God. Right away, Joan picked the king out of the crowd and approached him.

It was clear that there was something surprising about this girl.

The French armies were suffering defeat at every turn. So after Joan was examined by a group of priests to make sure that she was speaking from the heart and wasn't crazy, she was allowed to help command the French army.

When Joan joined the French army, she cut her hair short. She started wearing the kind of uniforms the male soldiers wore. Her uniform was a little different, though. It was all white, since Joan was a girl of great purity who listened to the voices of the saints and nothing else.

Amazingly enough, with Joan at the head of the troops, the French army defeated the English in several battles. After about a year, Charles VII was crowned king of France and took back the throne that was rightfully his.

The story isn't over, though. Some parts of France were still held by the English, and battles still raged. After some months of rest, Joan went back into battle. But this time, the ending was not a happy one.

The French were defeated, and Joan was captured. She was sold to the English. In a short time, her trial began.

The English had no real reason to put Joan on trial. But they had to find a reason to get rid of her—she was too powerful of an inspiration to the French. So the English worked closely with some bishops and priests in the area they controlled. Together, they put Joan on trial for heresy and witchcraft.

Before the trial, Joan was kept in terrible conditions. She was imprisoned along with male prisoners. She was kept in an iron cage, with her neck, hands, and feet chained to the bars. She was not allowed to go to Mass.

During the trial, she had to defend herself. The court wouldn't allow anyone else to represent her.

The records of the trial still exist. From them we can see that Joan defended herself with simplicity and grace, even though she was all alone among the enemy and even though none of those she had defended, including the king of France himself, ever came to her defense. She was accused of witchcraft because she said she heard voices. It didn't matter that Joan knew that the voices were those of good and holy saints. The court twisted her words, and she was accused of listening to evil spirits. She was accused of being one with the devil because she wore men's clothes in battle.

Joan was threatened with torture, but she wouldn't betray her voices. She was threatened with death, but she wouldn't betray her country. At the end of two long months, Joan was sentenced to death.

St. Joan of Arc

A stake was set up in the public square of a town called Rouen. Wood was piled high at the base of the stake, and Joan was brought out before the angry crowd. After she was tied to the stake, she asked for just one thing: a cross.

The cross was brought to Joan, and she held it in front of her. She started praying, saying the name of Jesus over and over. The wood beneath the stake was lit. It began to smoke slowly, and then it burst into crackling flames that started licking at Joan's feet. She still held the cross. She still called out the name of Jesus. She still proclaimed that the voices she heard were real and true.

Joan's ashes were thrown into the Seine, the river that runs through the middle of Paris. Twenty years after she died, the English were thrown out of France for good. Soon after that, another trial began. The records of Joan's case were reopened. Witnesses were called—including members of her own family. In the end, Joan of Arc was declared innocent.

Yes, it's easy to judge others. It's easy to decide what a person is like just from what she looks like on the outside. But as St. Joan of Arc shows us, you just never know what surprises are hiding inside.

St. Joan of Arc followed her conscience even though it brought her great suffering. What hard choices between right and wrong have you had to make?

St. Catherine of Siena *1347–1380*

April 29

Do you ever feel as if you don't fit in?

Do you like different kinds of television shows and music than those your friends like? Would some of your hobbies make other kids laugh and think you were a little strange? Is your family puzzled by some of the things that are important to you? Do they want to know why you just can't be like everyone else?

Many centuries ago, a young girl named Catherine spent her whole life answering that question. From the time she was very young, she surprised everyone. Nothing she did was normal or expected. Some of the things she did might even surprise you.

Even as a child, Catherine knew that what she wanted more than anything else was to be close to Jesus. Early in her life, she decided that the best way for her to put Jesus first was to never get married.

That was surprise number one. Her parents found it especially surprising. Catherine was their last living daughter (out of twenty-four children!) and of course they hoped she would get married and have a family of her own. Catherine stood firm. She knew she couldn't get married and still put God first.

Well, then, why not join a convent?

Catherine didn't want that either. It was true that if she became a nun, she would be able to concentrate on God. But she would also have to stay inside the convent every day and night for the rest of her life and pray in the ways that all the other nuns prayed. Catherine was certain that that wasn't what God wanted for her.

That was surprise number two. Today, women can do almost anything with their lives, but back in Italy during the fourteenth century, there weren't so many choices. Most women either got married or joined a convent. It was strange for a woman to decide that she wouldn't do either, but that's what Catherine had to do. She knew that her life couldn't be controlled by anyone's rules but God's.

But that's not all. Catherine had even more surprises.

Prayer was the most important part of Catherine's life, but some of the ways she prayed puzzled and even frightened people. Catherine didn't just pray with her heart. She prayed with her body too—her whole self.

She didn't eat much. Sometimes she ate nothing but a spoonful of herbs a day, and sometimes she couldn't even get that down. She drank water, though, and often depended on Jesus in the Eucharist for her food. She slept very little—sometimes only about thirty minutes a night—and on hard boards. She cut her hair very short and wore uncomfortable clothes.

Why in the world would anyone do this? You can imagine that her parents were upset and that the people in her town of Siena thought she was totally strange.

Catherine knew her way of praying wasn't for everyone. But maybe this will help you understand what Catherine was trying to do. When we pray, we concentrate on God. Catherine was concentrating her whole self—body and soul—on God.

Not very ordinary, is it?

Catherine didn't make the choices she made and didn't live in an unusual way just because she felt like it or because she liked making people mad. She did it because she knew God wanted her to do it. She knew that God had big plans for her. In order to carry out those plans, Catherine had to be free, strong, and close to God.

Why did she need to be free? So she could travel to France. Why did she need to be strong? Because she was going to tell the pope what to do!

Let's see how all this fits together.

You know that the pope is the leader of the Catholic Church. He's also the bishop of the city of Rome, so that's where he's supposed to live. But during Catherine's life, the French king controlled the pope, who had moved to a city called Avignon in France.

These were terrible times for the church. Leaders of different countries were trying to control the church. The pope was living in splendor, like a king himself. Christians everywhere were very confused. They weren't sure that the pope was really speaking for God anymore. The only way to start fixing things was for the pope to move back to Rome.

But he was afraid. He was afraid that the French and the other enemies would kill him if he left. Who would help him get the courage to do what was right?

That young woman who was always making people wonder— Catherine of Siena.

Catherine was just a young woman. She couldn't even read. But for years she had been leading this surprising life of prayer and had been teaching others about God. People all over Europe knew how close she was to God. When she spoke, they took her seriously.

So Catherine traveled to France to the elegant home of the pope. She stood, unafraid, before one of the most powerful leaders in Europe and told him what God had told her. He was to return to Rome and lead the church freely, as Jesus wanted him to do.

The pope listened. Late one night, in secret, the pope left France and returned to his home in Italy. Catherine followed soon after, going back to her own home to continue to pray and teach.

Catherine's life was full of surprises. She didn't fit into any box people wanted to squeeze her into. You may notice that about many of the people in this book!

Catherine's story tells us something very important. When we walk into the world, ready to tell everyone about God's love, the gifts that will be the most helpful to us are almost always the gifts that are the biggest surprises to other people!

St. Catherine of Siena didn't care about other people's opinions or expectations. The only opinion that mattered to her was God's. Can you think of times when you've had to follow your conscience and do the right thing even though other people discouraged you?

 # PART 4

People Who Create

In the beginning . . . God created the heavens and the earth.

Genesis 1:1

St. Hildegard of Bingen *1098–1179*

September 17

Stories, jokes, bits of music, rhymes—you come up with them all the time.

If you have time, you write them down, and if you're lucky, you'll find someone to share them with. The process goes something like this. You see a blank sheet of paper, and after just a few seconds of thought, you know how you want to fill it up. You draw mountains and forests, maybe even another planet. You draw aliens fighting or horses galloping in a field.

Or maybe you sit down at the piano and strike a key. You hit another, then another, and before you know it, you've made up a little tune.

It's all yours too. It came out of your spirit. It tells the world about what's going on inside of you.

You're creating!

Did you know that human beings are the only animals that really create? Yes, animals make things, but that's not the same as creating. A certain kind of bird only makes a certain kind of nest. She doesn't wake up in the morning and try to figure out how she's going to design her nest that day. She doesn't write a new tune to warble every day. Her designs and her tune are instincts given to her by God. That bird can't make anything new.

But you can make things up, all day and all night, in ways that no other person has done before. All of us can, because the power to create is a gift God gave us when he made us in his image. Whenever we use this gift of creativity, we're doing important work, hand in hand with God. It's work that can even bring holiness and grace into the world.

When we think of saints who were especially blessed with the gifts of creativity and imagination, one of the first to come to mind is Hildegard of Bingen.

Hildegard of Bingen was simply an amazing woman. She lived during the twelfth century. At a very young age, she was sent to live in a convent to be educated by an intelligent woman named Jutta.

Hildegard lived in that convent for almost twenty-five years, learning, doing hard work, and praying. When Jutta died, Hildegard was elected the abbess, or leader, of the sisters living in the convent. Soon after that, Hildegard decided to start her own convent. In her convent, nuns would lead a tougher life than the one they were used to. Hildegard moved up the river with several other nuns, and they settled there. They built a new place where women could live and work together, praying and giving glory to God.

That's impressive, but it's not all. It's not why we're telling Hildegard's story here.

Hildegard lived during the Middle Ages. She was one of the most creative people of her time. From the time she was a little girl, she had beautiful visions of heaven, the angels, and saints. She spent years writing long books in which she described the whole world as she understood it and saw it in her visions. She used all of the scientific knowledge of her time to describe how the world was made, what was in the heavens, and what was under the earth.

She described people too. She explained how she thought God put souls into our bodies. She thought a tongue of fire came down from heaven and filled us up while we were new in our mother's wombs. She wrote a book bringing together everything she knew about how to use plants and animals to heal illnesses.

Kings respected her wisdom and wrote to her for advice. Hildegard was very critical of some priests and bishops of her time who lived in far too much wealth and splendor. She wrote letters and spoke of how these Christian leaders should start living the simple life of Jesus. Although she was critical, or perhaps because she had the courage to speak out, those same bishops and priests, and even the pope, read her books and asked her for advice too.

Hildegard also wrote music. In fact, Hildegard was one of the earliest composers of music in Europe. She was certainly the first composer whose life we know anything about.

If you listen to Hildegard's music, you will hear pure, steady voices singing about God's powerful presence in all of creation. She wanted the voices to sound like angels singing. Her music was about Jesus' and God's love for us. She also wrote music about Mary and the other saints.

Because she lived in a convent, Hildegard wrote music for women's voices. She also wrote one of the earliest musical plays. In the play, which the nuns in the convent performed for each other, goodness and evil fought for power over a human soul.

Hildegard created beautiful music that lifts our spirits a bit closer to heaven. She used her imagination and her talents to share with the rest of us exactly what she saw and heard herself: the glory and the beauty of God.

St. Hildegard of Bingen wrote music to help others draw closer to God. What are you good at creating? How can what you create help people understand God's love?

Blessed Fra Angelico *1387–1455*

Everywhere you look, you can find beautiful things.

A clear, dark sky glittering with stars. A perfect rose. A sleek, spotted cheetah racing over African plains. A baby's tiny little toes. All beautiful, all gifts from God.

But people can make beautiful things too. Artists, composers, writers—even chefs, gardeners, and carpenters—all make beautiful things. They use their imaginations to create things that help us see what we can't see on our own.

Artists observe. They study the world. They think about it. They look at things again and again, a little closer and a little more deeply each time. Then artists use their paints, their words, or their musical notes to tell the rest of us about the beauty they've discovered.

Artists do special work. They point us in the direction of beauty. That means they're pointing us toward God, who is beauty, truth, goodness, and love.

Just try to imagine faith without art and music. There would be no paintings, no stained glass, no statues, and no holy cards. Every word would be spoken, and not a note would be sung in praise.

Do you see how important artists are?

Pope John Paul II, who wrote plays and poetry, knew this, and that's why he beatified (declared blessed) an artist in 1982 and named this man the patron saint of all artists.

The artist's name is Fra Angelico.

Fra Angelico lived in Italy during the fifteenth century. We know nothing at all about his childhood except that his name was Guido da Vicchio. When he was about twenty years old and already an excellent artist, Guido joined the Dominican order and took on a new name: Fra Giovanni, which means Friar John.

So why is he called Fra Angelico? As you might guess, *Angelico* means "angelic." That's exactly what this young artist was. He led a holy life, and he painted pictures that reminded everyone of heaven.

In those days, artists didn't usually work to sell their paintings in shops. Most art was created for churches and monasteries, and that's what Fra Angelico spent his whole life doing. He painted Jesus, Mary, the saints, and scenes from the Bible so that when people went to Mass, they could see beautiful pictures that would help them pray.

Many of Fra Angelico's paintings are what we call frescoes. A fresco is a picture painted directly on a wall that has been covered in wet plaster. Fra Angelico spent a great deal of time painting lovely frescoes in one particular monastery, San Marco, where he also lived. Even today, you can go to the monastery and see his frescoes. They can be found on almost every wall, including the walls of the monks' rooms!

When you look at one of Fra Angelico's frescoes or at any painting he created, you see calm, peaceful figures clothed in brightly colored robes that are trimmed in shimmering gold. You see stories and scenes from the Bible. You can easily understand them because Fra Angelico helps you, not with words, but with how he painted the people.

When Fra Angelico painted Jesus on the cross, he helped us understand suffering. But his paintings aren't filled with gore and tortured faces.

Fra Angelico's paintings of Jesus on the cross are very simple. Tiny rivulets of blood fall from Jesus' feet and hands, tracing a path down bare rock. His mother turns away in sadness. Another figure—maybe Saint Dominic, whom Fra Angelico liked to put in his paintings—buries his face in his hands.

That simple sorrow tells us all we need to know about Jesus' pain and his love for us.

Fra Angelico believed that in order to really portray Christ, a person must be Christlike. It's said that Fra Angelico always prayed before starting his work, and it shows. His paintings are filled with the calm peace of a person who is absolutely sure that God is love.

One of his friends said of Fra Angelico, "No one could paint like that without first having been to heaven."

What does that mean?

It means that artists create what they see. And if an artist is close to God, he'll see God in the world. He'll see a world that's beautiful, not just because it's pretty, but because it shows us God's beauty too.

Fra Angelico was an artist like that. His paintings are filled with God's light and God's love. Fra Angelico served God by bringing more beauty into the world. What beautiful thing can you create today?

Fra Angelico tried to reflect the beauty of God's love in what he created. When you create something, what are you trying to express?

St. John of the Cross *1542–1591*

December 14

What's your favorite kind of story to read?

Do you like mysteries? funny books? Do you like stories about people who lived long ago or about beings that might live on other planets? Do you like to curl up with a book of poems?

Aren't you grateful for all of your favorite authors? Just imagine what a boring world it would be without their words and stories.

We like stories for a lot of reasons. We like them because they're funny or scary. We like finding out how the mystery is solved. We like to see our hero come out all right in the end.

Good stories, poems, and plays always help us feel more at home in the world. Good authors help us understand life a little better.

That's why authors write stories in the first place. Like other artists, they see something important that they want to share with other people. Then they use characters and scenes to show us.

Maybe a writer wants to show us how interesting life is in other lands. Maybe she wants us to read a story about kids just like us so we know we're not alone. Maybe she hopes that her stories will show us how important it is to feel happy with ourselves. Can you think of some things you've learned in stories?

Now, if a writer believes in God, that belief adds even more to the story the writer wants to tell. The world isn't just about people and plants and animals. It's about God too. And a writer who loves God will help readers see and understand God.

This is what St. John of the Cross did. He didn't write stories, exactly. He wrote poems. We know that he also wrote music and made sculptures and paintings, but none of this work has survived over the past four hundred years.

John of the Cross was a leader too. He taught many people how to pray and be closer to God. Those things were certainly important, but we remember John here as the saint who was a poet.

John was a small man. His family was quite poor, and John never had much food to eat when he was a child. That stunted his growth, so he was only about five feet tall.

He lived in Spain during the sixteenth century. After some years of study at a university, John decided he wanted to become a monk. He decided he wanted to lead the humblest life he possibly could. He wanted to live so that God would be all he had to depend on.

During John's time, some monasteries were comfortable places, but that's not what John wanted. Why join a monastery if it was going to be a life of ease? He joined a religious order that was simple and rather hard. Soon, though, he met someone who told him about an even simpler way of life. This new acquaintance was Teresa of Ávila.

You can read about St. Teresa of Ávila elsewhere in this book (page 85). She was a Spanish nun who worked hard to help orders of sisters live more humbly and more focused on Jesus. She met John, who was many years younger than she was, and she was very impressed with him. John was young, but he led a holy life. Teresa asked John to help her start new, simpler houses for monks and nuns.

John agreed, but he soon found himself in trouble.

Many monks were angered by what Teresa and John were trying to do. They were afraid that Teresa and John would try to make all the monasteries embrace that simpler style of life.

They weren't trying to do that, of course, but that didn't matter. The monks were so angry that they did something terrible. They kidnapped John.

That's right. The monks kidnapped John of the Cross and took him to another town. They threw him into a cell that was only about ten feet long and six feet wide. The cell had only a slit for a window.

They kept John there for nine months. They fed him bread, water, and sardines. Every day after their prayers they let him out to ask him if he had changed his mind about the new monasteries. He always said no, so every day he was whipped with a heavy rope. These whippings left scars on his shoulders that would be there for the rest of his life.

John lived in that tiny, filthy, dark cell for almost a year. He had nothing to write with and nothing to do but pray. So pray is what John did.

At times he felt alone and abandoned, even by God. But he kept praying. At times he wondered why he had followed God at all. But he kept praying.

And there in the dark, John wrote poems in his head.

In beautiful Spanish, John wrote poems about God and God's love. He wrote poems about how God's love is always with you, even if you're suffering and even if you can't feel that love.

It seemed that John might never get out of his prison. It seemed that he might never have a chance to write his poems down and help Teresa. But one dark, cold night, one of the guards looked the other way, and John took his chance. He tied his bedclothes together and hung them out a window like a rope. He climbed down to the ground and rushed to the nearest church. He was free!

John rushed back to Teresa of Ávila. He went back to helping the monasteries follow Jesus more closely. And he wrote down his poems.

John's poems are some of the greatest poems ever written in the Spanish language. People love them because they are good poetry. But people also love them because they are like any good story: they help us understand the world.

John's poems help us understand that suffering is a part of life. They help us see that even when we suffer, God is with us. They help us understand that if we hang on to God's love, nothing can ever really hurt us.

Do you know that every book you open is a present? It's a present from the writer. He worked hard on it and spent a lot of time writing it. He might have even told you about a part of his own life when he wrote the story for you to enjoy. He's giving you a gift from the very deepest part of himself.

That's what St. John of the Cross did. He suffered a lot, but he survived. Even more amazing, the awful things that happened to John helped him write poetry that has helped millions of people love God more and get through their own times of suffering and loneliness.

Now that's a gift to be grateful for, isn't it?

When St. John of the Cross was suffering the most, he used that suffering to write beautiful poems about God. Are there ways that you can help others by using what you learn about yourself when you're sad?

Blessed Miguel Pro *1891–1927*

November 23

Do you know someone who's just full of energy and ideas?

This person is probably always working on lots of projects. Maybe he's playing music, writing stories, or organizing everybody else to play a prank. You don't know how he does it all, but you know you're really glad when he walks into the room.

Or maybe that person is you. Is it? Do you wish there were more hours in the day so you could dance more, be in more plays, or draw more pictures? If this is how you are, then you are blessed. You're creative!

We can do a lot with God's gift of creativity. We can make people laugh. We can help people understand the world. And we can always and everywhere use these gifts for God's glory.

Miguel Pro was a very creative person. If you'd been in Miguel's class in school, he would have been the boy who made everyone giggle with his imitations of the teacher. He would have been the one who drew funny cartoons for the school newspaper. He would have been the star of the class play.

Miguel was born in Mexico a little more than a hundred years ago. He was part of a large, loving family. When he was a young boy, he went to school sometimes, and sometimes he was taught at home.

When Miguel decided to study to become a priest, he was always the center of fun among his classmates. He went to school in

Mexico, the United States, and Europe. He wrote articles and stories for the school papers. He loved to draw cartoons too.

But almost more than anything else, Miguel enjoyed putting on and acting in plays. In those days before television, the students often put on plays for each other. Miguel was such a good mimic that he could play any part.

It wasn't all fun and games, though. Through all of those years of study, Miguel worked hard. He grew closer to Jesus. He gave much of his time to helping the poor and the sick. When he lived in Europe, he talked with many people about ways they could help poor people have better lives. But Miguel wanted to be able to help the poor in his own country too. He knew he would be going back to Mexico soon, and he was ready.

Finally, the day came. Miguel was ordained a priest. He would soon get on a ship, return to his home, and serve his people.

Miguel could hardly wait, even though he knew that Mexico was facing hard times. Those hard times had started even before he left, and they'd only gotten worse during the years he was away.

There had been a revolution in Mexico. For years, wars and battles had raged. When peace finally came, something else came with it: new rulers of Mexico who hated the church. They hated it so much that they destroyed churches and statues. They made it a crime to go to Mass or to teach children about Jesus. If Miguel Pro went back to Mexico and followed his dream, he would be breaking the law.

So he went without a second thought.

He went back even though it was terribly dangerous. He went back because he knew that the people of Mexico needed God and that no matter what their rulers said, they wanted God. They wanted to receive Jesus in the Eucharist. They wanted their children baptized. They wanted to be able to pray and learn about Jesus.

Miguel knew that helping his people keep their faith was more important than his own safety.

Miguel had always been creative. At home and in school, he never ran out of ideas. When he arrived in Mexico, Miguel saw right away that he was going to have to be creative again. He was going to have to think on his feet. He was going to have to act. He was going to have to tell stories. Why?

Because if Miguel was going to serve his people as a priest, he would have to do it in secret. If he didn't, Miguel would be arrested, just for saying Mass. And all the people with him would be arrested too.

Miguel Pro was going to have to be more creative than he had ever been before. He was going to have to use all of that courage and imagination to protect himself and God's people, all for God's glory.

Here's what Miguel did.

The Mexican rulers had closed the churches for worship, so Miguel had to say Mass in people's homes. He couldn't wear the regular priest's clothing, of course. He wore whatever would help him fit in that day. Miguel wore simple worker's clothing or a suit with a jaunty straw hat.

If the police suspected that he might be a priest, Miguel had to think quickly in order to escape. He had to be ready to use his imagination and act a part at any time.

Once, the police followed him and almost trapped him on a dead-end street. A young woman Miguel knew happened to be walking down the same street. Miguel took her arm and pretended to be her boyfriend!

Another time, Miguel came to the house where he was supposed to say Mass that day. Two police officers were standing in front. Miguel immediately knew what to do. He took out a notepad, wrote down the number of the house, and pretended he had a badge under his coat lapel. He was pretending to be a policeman! That way, he could go into the house and say Mass, with the police standing right out front, thinking he was one of them and that he was searching the house for a criminal priest!

Miguel's creativity worked. For about a year, Miguel Pro worked in secret in Mexico City. He said Mass. He gave communion to those who couldn't leave their homes. He organized a vast system of giving food and clothing to the hungry. He even gave retreats, completely in secret, to hundreds of people!

It couldn't last, though. One day in November of 1927, a man tried to kill an important general. The man escaped. But the police found the car he'd used. They traced it to Humberto Pro, Miguel's brother.

Humberto had not had anything to do with the attempted killing, but that didn't matter. The police arrested him and two of his brothers, including Miguel, whom they were very glad to find because he was a priest.

The police didn't plan a trial for Miguel, only an execution.

Miguel was ready. He knew that serving God in those days would probably bring death. He was ready to stand up for the truth.

On the morning of his execution, the guards walked Miguel out to the prison yard. They offered him a blindfold, but he refused. All he wanted was a moment to pray.

After Miguel prayed, he stood up. He held a crucifix in one hand and a rosary in the other. Miguel spread his arms out by his sides. He wanted to die just as Jesus had died.

The firing squad held their rifles. Miguel moved his lips, and those nearby heard his words. He proclaimed that Christ would live forever, no matter what.

"Viva Christo Rey!"

The guns fired, and Miguel Pro fell to the earth, killed for serving God's people.

All of us can be creative. All of us can use our imaginations. We can use our talents to make people laugh, just as Miguel Pro did during his school days. And maybe when we think about Blessed Miguel Pro, we'll decide to use our gift of creativity to do the most important work of all. And that's bringing the love of Jesus into the lives of everyone we meet, in whatever ways our imaginations take us.

Blessed Miguel Pro was creative, and just as important, he was brave enough to use that creative talent to help others in danger. Can you think of some ways to use your creative talents to help others, even though it might be difficult or require sacrifice?

PART 5

SAINTS ARE

People Who Teach Us New Ways to Pray

Lord, teach us to pray.

Luke 11:1

St. Benedict *480–547*

July 11

When times are bad, we have to stick together, don't we?

If a big storm is on its way, we have to work with others to get all the supplies we need. People who are strong have to help people who can't do as much for themselves. If something really sad happens in our school or to our family—if someone dies or is in a terrible accident—we have to forget our differences and try to help each other understand and be strong.

In fact, when we come together during hard times, we often discover how much we've needed other people all along.

We need other people to teach us about life. We need to combine our gifts and talents with those of other people to make the world a better place. Working with others makes life easier. It's more fun too.

St. Benedict's life was all about teaching people how important it is to stick together. He understood that life falls apart when people just go their own way.

When Benedict was a young boy in Italy during the fifth century, times were very hard for everyone. The country had endured terrible wars for years and years. People were poor, and they had few strong leaders. Every day was a struggle just to survive. The government collapsed, and people were on their own.

Benedict saw how terrible this was. Because life was so hard and people were facing it on their own, they were becoming selfish. They didn't think they had enough time to pray, so they were leaving God out of their lives. The world was becoming a scary, lonely place.

When Benedict was an adult, he became a monk. He lived as a monk for three years, and one day he decided that starting his own monasteries could help. A monastery is a place where monks live, work, and pray together. Monks are men, but women can live that way too. If they do, their home is usually called a convent, and the women are called nuns.

Benedict's plan to start his own monasteries was a good idea. In his monasteries, men could work together instead of just farming for themselves, which was difficult during those hard times. That way, they could produce more crops. Some people made clothes, other people built things, and others cooked. Everyone had a job to do, but no one person had to do everything. The monasteries became places of calm, happy work.

But work took up only part of the day. Benedict didn't want his monks to ever forget that God was the most important part of life and that we can't be strong unless we're close to God. So Benedict had his monks spend hours every day praying and reading the Bible. Most of the time they didn't do these things by themselves. For hours each day, the monks came together in their chapels to chant the psalms, listen to the Bible, and sit together in quiet reflection.

Prayer and work. Benedict understood very clearly that this was what people needed in those hard times. They needed to pray and work together, thanking God the whole time for all his gifts.

There are lots of stories about Benedict that tell us that he was an understanding man. He could see into people's hearts and understand just what they needed in order to be happy.

Once, before he had started his own monasteries, Benedict was asked to be the leader of some monks who weren't too serious about the way they were living. He agreed, although he knew it probably wouldn't work out.

He was right. In fact, the situation turned out so badly that the monks completely turned against him. They were so angry that they even tried to kill Benedict! This is what happened.

Benedict sat down to dinner with the other monks, who were watching him very carefully. They had a plan to take care of Benedict once and for all. One of the monks put a cup of wine in front of Benedict. As he usually did before he ate or drank anything, Benedict blessed it.

The monks waited. As Benedict made the sign of the cross over the cup, a shocking thing happened. It shattered right in front of their eyes! The wine, which you've probably guessed was poisoned, spilled onto the table. Benedict turned to the monks and shook his head.

"I told you we wouldn't get along," he said. "Go get a leader that you want to obey. May God forgive you for trying to hurt me!"

Benedict had read the monks' hearts, and many other stories tell us how well Benedict understood other people.

No other monks ever tried to kill Benedict after that. Instead, they came to him in great numbers, wanting to lead simple lives of work and prayer. That's when he decided to start his own monasteries.

In his monasteries, Benedict planted little seeds—seeds of working and praying together—that grew and grew. Thousands of monasteries were founded on his plan, which is called a Rule. During the Middle Ages, when Europe was facing very difficult times, the monasteries kept faith, learning, and hope alive.

Benedict understood that we're strongest when we depend on each other. He understood that God gave us life and that thanking

God for that life should be the reason behind every word we speak and every bit of work we do. He understood that great things can happen when we're all working and praying together.

So what do you say? Instead of trying to do everything all by yourself, why not open the door to your bedroom, find a reason to share a smile and a bit of God's love, and try working with others?

St. Benedict taught his monks that God is glorified when we all work together. What are some ways that you need other people to help you understand and live God's love?

St. Dominic de Guzman *1170–1221*

August 8

What helps you pray?

Do you have a crucifix or a holy card that reminds you of Jesus? Do you read the Bible? When you're in church, do the statues, songs, and stained-glass windows help you keep your mind on God's love?

Praying isn't always easy. Our minds may wander. We may be unsure of what to say. We may just be learning that an important part of prayer is having a quiet spirit and listening to God.

That's why we have things to help us. We have songs, pictures, and stories. We have saints in stained glass, statues, and candles.

And we have the rosary.

No one knows exactly how the rosary began. It might have come from a tradition that monks had in ancient times. Hundreds of years ago, an important part of a monk's prayer life was praying the psalms. The monks would pray together, and every week they would manage to pray aloud all 150 psalms.

Everyone knew this was a wonderful way to pray. But people who didn't live in convents or monasteries—people who worked in the fields or in the towns—didn't have time to say all of the psalms.

But since they knew other, shorter prayers already, they could repeat those prayers often. They could say the Hail Mary. Then they could add the Lord's Prayer, the Apostle's Creed, and the Hail, Holy

Queen. And they could keep track of which prayers they prayed and how many times they prayed them by putting beads on a string, each bead representing a certain prayer. This formed what we now call the rosary.

After many centuries the rosary developed into what we know it as today. It was a set of beads that helped people say 150 prayers, the same number of prayers that the monks said in the monastery.

Now, you know that your rosary doesn't have 150 beads. Your rosary has 59 beads on which you can say the Hail Mary and the other prayers. Your rosary is really just one-third of a full rosary, but that's okay. If you want to see a full rosary, you have to look someplace special.

The one place you're sure to find that long, full rosary is on the waist of a Dominican priest, brother, or sister. The Dominican order was founded by a Spanish man named Dominic who lived around the same time as St. Francis of Assisi, whom you can read about later in this book (page 205). The rosary has always been a very important prayer for Dominicans, and here's why.

When he was a young priest, Dominic was given a special but difficult job. It was a job other people had tried to do but had failed at. It was a job that was dangerous as well as challenging.

In parts of France, a strange belief had taken hold among the people. It was called Albigensianism. Albigensians believed that the body and all other matter were evil. They believed that Jesus wasn't really human. In fact, they believed that he hadn't ever been born. They believed that marriage was bad and having babies was bad. Since they believed that everything about life except the spirit was evil, they taught that suicide was good.

For some reason, this belief had become very popular, and the church was at its wits end trying to stop it. Dominic was called in to help.

Dominic did everything he could. He preached and taught, trying to show the people how silly these beliefs were. He debated their leaders and teachers.

More than anything else, Dominic prayed.

He knew that one of the reasons this odd belief had become popular was that the church's own leaders had sinned. Many of them lived in luxury, and some even sinned openly. People found it really hard to believe anything these leaders said.

Dominic knew that the people wouldn't listen unless they were taught by actions as well as by words.

Dominic lived simply. The others who gathered to help him, the men who became the first Dominicans, lived simply too. They prayed all the time, in private and in front of other people.

And they prayed the rosary.

Many years after St. Dominic died, a book was written about him. In that book, the author tells a story about St. Dominic and the rosary.

In the story, it's said that Dominic was completely frustrated by the Albigensians. He had argued and preached until he could hardly talk anymore. He didn't know where to turn next, so he decided to go off and pray for a few days.

Dominic found a cave, hidden deep in a nearby forest. For three days, he prayed and fasted in the darkness of that cave, asking God for the strength and the wisdom to go on. These beliefs he was fighting were terribly dangerous, and they were keeping people from the joy of Jesus' love. What could Dominic do?

Deep in prayer, he received his answer. The answer came from Mary, the mother of Jesus. Dominic saw her coming to him, right there in that cave, with three angels at her side.

Mary spoke gently to Dominic. She told him that she knew the peoples' eyes and ears were closed and that their hearts were hardened. She said that the only way to get through to them was with the rosary.

So that's what Dominic started to do. When he preached, he took those beads and showed the people how to use them. He prayed it with them, wherever he was, under any kind of roof.

Finally, the rosary began to open hearts in a way nothing else had.

Of course, nothing happens all at once, and the Albigensian beliefs didn't completely die out for many years. But many people returned to God's love because of the rosary. When Dominic used the rosary, he was showing the people that the things of this earth aren't bad. God made the world. God made us. Nature and even things that come from human hands can help us draw closer to God.

We have pictures of our friends to remind us of fun times. We have a special little toy our parents gave us long ago, and when we pick it up and hold it, if only for a second, we're reconnected to our parents, even if they're not in the room.

St. Dominic knew that we sometimes need help when we pray. We need solid things to help us remember and concentrate. That's exactly what those beads do. They're not magic, and they're not good luck charms either. Those little round bits of glass or wood are solid things. When we hold them between our fingers while we say our prayers at night, we're letting our whole self—body and soul—rest in God's love.

St. Dominic helped people understand that prayer involves our bodies as well as our souls. What can you see, feel, and touch around your house that reminds you of God's love?

St. Teresa of Ávila *1515–1582*

October 15

Friends are really important, aren't they?

We do lots of things with our friends. We play games, we go to the movies, and we do school projects with our friends. We have sleepovers and join the same baseball or soccer teams.

We also talk with our friends. After all, how in the world can you be friends with someone if you don't talk to each other?

It's the same way with God. If we want to be friends with God, we have to talk to him. We have to listen too.

That kind of talking is called prayer.

Prayer is a lot like friendship. As you grow older, friendship changes. When you're little, you and your friends don't do much more than get together and play games. When you get older, you do all of that and more. Talking and listening to each other, helping each other with problems, and just wondering together about all the weird stuff that goes on in the world are all great parts of friendship.

Prayer changes too. When you're little, most of your praying is talking to God in words you've memorized. There's nothing wrong with that. When you're eighty years old, you'll still be talking to God that way, getting close to God by whispering words you learned when you were five.

But there's more to your praying. The older you get, the more you see that when you pray, you don't just *talk* to God. You *listen.* And when you get right down to it, what you're really trying to do is just be with God and be filled with his love.

Sound hard? Well, it's harder than making a sandwich, but it's not much harder than forming a really close friendship. Lots of people have done it, and lots of people have spent their lives helping others learn how to do it too.

Teresa of Ávila was one of those people. Now, if you're thinking that someone who knows a lot about prayer must be a boring person who sits in a room all day with her eyes shut, think again. Teresa of Ávila was anything but that.

From the very beginnings of her life in the town of Ávila, Spain, Teresa was full of energy. One day, when she was only about seven years old, Teresa had an idea. In those days, many Christians in Spain were still afraid of people called Moors. The Moors lived across the Mediterranean Sea in Africa, and for hundreds of years, the Moors and the Spanish had been fighting.

Little Teresa had heard many terrible stories about how the Moors treated Christians, but she wasn't afraid of them. In fact, she thought it would be marvelous if she and her brother just went to Africa to tell the Moors about Jesus. It didn't bother her one bit that she might get killed. She liked the idea of giving her life for Jesus.

Her brother wasn't as excited, but he went along anyway. They packed sacks with bread and a few other supplies and started on their way, through the narrow streets of Ávila, out through the city gate (most towns were built with walls around them at that time), and along the rough dirt road that led south.

Of course, they didn't get very far. Before long, their uncle dashed after them and brought the two children back. Teresa's brother didn't hesitate to put all the blame on her.

But that probably didn't bother Teresa. She was ready to work hard for God, no matter what people said.

Teresa became a nun when she was just twenty years old. In those days, many nuns in Spain led pretty easy lives. For a long time, Teresa was happy with this. But as she grew older, she began to pray more and draw closer to God. Her time with God could get so intense that if other people were around, Teresa wouldn't know they were there. All she would feel was God, and sometimes, deep within her heart, she would see Jesus, Mary, and the angels as well.

By the time she was about forty years old, Teresa's praying had helped her see that the life she was leading was too easy. She believed that God wanted her to lead a simpler life.

So Teresa left her convent and started a new one. She and her sisters lived very humbly, saw few visitors, and spent a great deal of time studying and praying. Teresa even wanted her sisters to dress more plainly, so they agreed to not wear shoes!

This was a tough sacrifice, especially in cold winters and hot summers and on rocky Spanish soil. After a short time, the sisters began to wear sandals, but this was still a much harder life than most people, even most nuns, lived.

Teresa worked very hard. She kept traveling around Spain even though she was in poor health and even though many people, including church leaders, opposed the changes she was making. She founded new convents almost until the day she died.

How did she do it?

First, Teresa was happy and had a sense of humor. Once, her carriage broke down, and she was thrown outside into the rain and mud. "If this is how you treat your friends, no wonder you have so few!" she said to God.

Second, Teresa and God were best friends. (That's why she could say things like that!) We're lucky because Teresa wrote several books explaining how we can all be best friends with God.

Teresa explained this using words and stories that anyone could understand. She wrote many books, and in one of them she said that letting God into your heart is like letting him plant seeds in your life. When we pray and help others, we help the seeds grow.

In another book, Teresa said that becoming friends with God is like walking through the rooms of a house. God is in the innermost room of the house, calling you to come to him. The outer rooms are filled with all kinds of things—like spider webs, snakes, and darkness—that can prevent you from hearing his voice. If you want to reach the place where God is, you have to get past the dangers in all of those other rooms first.

What would we do without friends? And what would we do without people like St. Teresa of Ávila, the woman who taught us how to be best friends with God?

St. Teresa of Ávila taught us what prayer really is: being with God, our best friend. When you pray, what do you do? Are you talking and listening to your best friend?

St. Louis de Monfort *1673–1716*

April 28

Isn't it weird that kids make fun of each other for being good?

Isn't it strange that kids make each other feel uncomfortable for doing the right thing? And isn't it odd that some kids can make it seem as if putting God first turns you into a goofball?

Don't worry. If that's the way you feel sometimes, you're not alone. In fact, you've never been alone. Even Jesus was misunderstood—just because he wanted to love and please God. Seeing faith in others often makes people uncomfortable.

Louis de Monfort lived in a time when religion was definitely not cool. He lived in France four hundred years ago, when there were churches on practically every block. But yet it wasn't all right to have strong faith in Jesus.

Sound familiar?

Louis de Monfort didn't really care what other people thought. You might have noticed that saints rarely do.

Louis was a great big man who'd spent many years studying for the priesthood. During those years, Louis learned a lot and grew very close to Jesus. When he became a priest, Louis made an important decision. He wanted to live as Jesus had lived.

Louis didn't want to live in one parish. He wanted to travel around, as Jesus had. Louis didn't want to stay locked up in an office. He wanted to wander, preach, and serve the poor, just as Jesus had.

So Louis got permission—from the pope himself!—and began his work.

It wasn't easy. First of all, the poor of France were suffering greatly in many ways. The rich didn't do much to help them, and in some towns the church itself wasn't doing a good job of helping and teaching the poor. In the places Louis visited, hardly anyone went to Mass or even knew how to start praying. Louis decided he would teach them.

At first, Louis almost always met with anger from the people he wanted to help. He was traveling in rough neighborhoods, and sometimes Louis had to be rough himself in order to get people's attention.

Once, Louis was preaching in a church that was next door to a tavern. All the doors and windows were open, and the men in the tavern didn't even try to be quiet. As they drank, they got louder and louder. Through the open windows, they made fun of the people in church. They also made fun of Louis.

Louis kept calm until the end of his preaching. Then he slowly walked out the church door and into the tavern. The men sitting at their wooden tables in the dark, smoky room looked at him, grinning, as if to say, Who needs God?

Louis stood and looked at the men. He knew that quiet words would be lost here. So would a gentle discussion.

Louis rolled up his sleeves and got to work. He turned over tables, spilled mugs and pitchers, and threw chairs against the wall. He knocked down a few of the men, broke some glasses, and walked out.

The next day, the tavern was quiet. The men from the tavern sat in church, listening to Louis and learning how to pray.

Another time, a public square was full of loud people drinking, dancing, and playing music—on a Sunday morning! As Louis approached, he noticed that the music everyone was dancing to was from a hymn he'd written himself. The musicians were actually putting bad words to music he'd written to praise God, and on a Sunday morning to boot!

Louis didn't wait. He grabbed the instruments and held a crucifix high in the air. He told everyone to stop celebrating their sins and to turn back to God. Two big men with swords marched toward Louis, ready to strike. He turned to them with fire in his eyes, still holding the crucifix high in the air. The men dropped their swords and ran the other way.

It wasn't that Louis didn't want people to have fun and enjoy life. He did. But he was worried because the people he met had tried to replace God with fun. Louis knew that fun doesn't last. It always ends. God's peace doesn't end—it's with you in the good times and the bad. Louis wanted people to put God first so they would be filled with his love, stop being so selfish, and take better care of each other.

Louis had another special message. He wanted people to know how important Mary is.

Whenever Louis preached and taught, he brought rosaries and taught people how to say that special prayer. He knew that Jesus came because Mary said yes to God. He wanted people to learn from Mary so they could say yes to God too.

The people Louis tried to help thought religion was stupid. They thought that games and fun gave them all the happiness they needed. They thought that the best way to live was to live for themselves.

Louis taught them to see religion in a new way. He was proud of God's love and would talk about it all day, as loudly as he could! He walked right into dangerous places to tell people about God. People laughed and made fun of him, but Louis didn't care.

And do you know what? It worked.

Because faith in God had made Louis strong and loving, people understood that God is that way too. When we're timid and quiet about our faith, of course people are going to think that God is for wimps and is not cool at all. When we're proud and confident of God's love, people start to see him in a new way.

You don't have to turn over tables, as Louis de Monfort did. You'd probably better not, as a matter of fact. But I'm sure you can think of another way you can help someone see how cool God really is.

St. Louis de Monfort tried to help people see how important God is. In your family, does God come first?

 **PART 6**

SAINTS ARE

People Who See beyond the Everyday

Blessed are your eyes, because they see, and your ears, because they hear.

Matthew 13:16

St. Juan Diego *1474–1548*

December 9

Friends are an important part of life, aren't they?

You probably have all kinds of friends. A few of them are close friends you've known for a long time. Some of them are people you go to school with or play sports with who maybe aren't so close to you but are still your friends.

But have you ever looked at a person for the first time and thought to yourself, "Well, that person can't be my friend because . . ."? You might have all kinds of reasons for thinking this. You might think the other person is too smart or not smart enough. You might think that he or she dresses differently than your other friends. The person might come from a different country or family background.

Whatever the reason, you might find that you've put up a wall between yourself and that person. You didn't really do it on purpose, and when you think about it, you're even a little ashamed. But the wall is still there. How can you take it down?

Maybe a good way to start is to see this other person not with your own eyes but with God's eyes. When God looks at this boy or girl, what does he see? Does he see someone who's "different," or does he see his own beloved child, loved just as much as you are?

Understanding how God's love touches everyone can take a long time. We can be thankful that God gives us plenty of chances to learn and comes into our world to teach us that lesson again and again. One of the most powerful ways God brought this message into the world was through a man named Juan Diego who lived hundreds of years ago.

On a chilly December morning in 1531, Juan Diego walked over the hills of his Mexican homeland to go to Mass. This wasn't so unusual. After all, Juan Diego walked to Mass every Saturday and Sunday morning. It was nine miles each way, but he didn't mind. During the seven years Juan Diego had been a Christian, he had grown very close to Jesus. Receiving Jesus in the Eucharist gave Juan Diego peace and strength.

Juan Diego was an Aztec Indian. His ancestors had lived in Mexico for centuries, perhaps even thousands of years. Until recently, Juan Diego and his people had lived under the rule of the Aztec tribe. The Aztecs were quite intelligent, but they could also be extremely cruel. Aztecs worshiped many gods, and they believed that these gods demanded sacrifice—even the lives of human beings. Every year, thousands of men, women, and children were killed in the great stone temples of Mexico as part of Aztec worship.

But a few years before Juan Diego's December walk, Spanish soldiers had come from across the sea and had conquered the Aztecs. The Spanish could be cruel themselves, and over the centuries many people suffered from diseases and other hardships brought by the conquistadors, or Spanish soldiers. But they did bring one good, life-saving thing to the people of Mexico: the good news of Jesus Christ.

Like many others, Juan Diego heard the good news. He was taught and baptized by a kind missionary. His new faith gave him strength for his simple but sometimes hard daily life as a weaver and farmer.

So on that winter morning, Juan Diego walked to church, so happy to be a Christian that he was willing to travel nine miles on foot just to receive Jesus in communion.

At the top of a hill, Juan Diego stopped. Something strange was going on. The songs of birds burst through the air, louder and more beautiful than he'd ever heard. And then he heard something else. It was a human voice, the voice of a woman. And it spoke not the Spanish of the conquerors, not the Latin of the church, but Juan's very own native language—the language of the poor people of Mexico.

"Juanito," the voice said, calling to him as if he were a beloved little son. "Juan Dieguito."

He climbed the hill toward the voice, and what he saw amazed him. A woman, dressed as an Aztec princess, glittered and glowed in the sun. She spoke again, asking Juan Diego where he was going. To church, he answered.

The lady told Juan Diego that she was the Virgin Mary. She asked Juan to go straightaway to the bishop and ask him to build a church on that very spot. Why? So that all of Juan Diego's people, all those who suffered, might have a place that would remind them of God's love.

Juan Diego was stunned, but he hurried on to the bishop's palace. The bishop agreed to see him, and Juan told him what he had seen. But since the bishop was a terribly busy man, he told Juan Diego it would be better to come back later with the whole story, in detail.

The next day, Juan Diego journeyed again to the city. In the same spot on the same hill, the Virgin appeared again. Juan told her what had happened with the bishop and begged her to find someone else to deliver her message.

Full of humility, Juan Diego said he was just "a small rope, a tiny ladder, the tail end, a leaf." Surely there was someone more powerful and educated, someone the bishop and other important people would take seriously.

"No," the Virgin said. No one but Juan Diego could deliver the message.

Once more, Juan Diego delivered to the bishop the Virgin's message. The bishop listened, but the story was hard to believe. He ordered Juan Diego to return the next day, but this time with proof.

Can you imagine how frustrated Juan Diego must have felt? How could he prove to the bishop that what he had seen was real?

The answer came the next day. As he approached the hill, he saw another surprising sight. There, in December, amid rocks and brambles, roses were blooming. Hundreds of roses! Roses never blossomed that time of year. Quickly, Juan Diego opened his tilm a (his cloak) and filled it with roses.

He rushed to the bishop's palace, carefully guarding the precious blooms. He stood before the bishop and opened his tilma. The roses tumbled out onto the floor, and the bishop's eyes opened wide with surprise. But Juan Diego noticed that the bishop wasn't looking at the roses. He was looking at Juan Diego's tilma.

Juan Diego looked down too. Imprinted on the humble patch of cloth he had woven himself was something he never expected to see: the Virgin.

A blue, starry veil was draped over her head and hung down her shoulders. Her hands were folded in prayer, and she stood in front of the sun and on top of a dark crescent. It was Jesus' mother.

The bishop knew then that every word Juan Diego had spoken was true. He did what Mary had asked and built a church on the spot where she had appeared, which you can visit today, just as millions of other people do every year. They visit the church to wonder at the miraculous image of Mary on Juan Diego's tilma, the image that we call "Our Lady of Guadalupe." When they see the tilma, they're reminded of the very important message that God gave us through this gift to Juan Diego: God's love and peace are for all people, rich and poor, all over this world he's made.

St. Juan Diego

God's gift to Juan Diego showed the leaders of the church in Mexico how much God loves all people. Do you sometimes forget that God loves all the people around you just as much as he loves you?

St. Frances of Rome *1384–1440*

March 9

Have you ever noticed that the older you get, the more you see?

I don't mean that your eyesight gets better. I just mean that you notice more—don't you?

When you were really little, you never saw much more than the toys on the floor in front of you or the oatmeal on your spoon. As you got older, you noticed a little more. You knew when you were in a new place. You started to look up at the sky and find pictures in the clouds.

When you were little, you looked at a painting and saw nothing more than a picture of a girl. Now, you notice the girl's expression. You can see the brushstrokes on the canvas. You can even see how this artist's painting is different from another artist's painting hanging on the same wall.

When you were little, you came into a room and all you could see was people. Some were big and some were small. Some were friends and some were strangers.

Now you can see a bit more. You notice how different people are. You notice which people are standing next to each other. You also notice which people stay as far away from each other as they can.

You're starting to see more, aren't you? You're seeing more of the stuff that's around you. You're also seeing why it's there, what it's for, and how it connects to you and to everything else.

It takes practice to see that way. It takes maturity and understanding. Your eyes have to be wide open to catch everything that's there. Your spirit has to be wide open too!

That's one thing that saints do: they see. They see the world—not just what it looks like on the surface, but what's underneath the surface. They see the world, but they see something else too: God, who's present in and through all the wonders he has made.

St. Frances of Rome saw all of that. She had eyes that took in everything around her. She saw what everyone else could see, and more.

Frances was born in Rome during the fifteenth century. As was common for girls in those days, a marriage was arranged for Frances when she was very young. She was supposed to get married when she was twelve years old!

Frances wasn't crazy about the idea. She had decided as an even younger girl that she wanted to be a nun, but her father wouldn't hear of it. The boy she was supposed to marry was handsome, kind, and religious. Of course she would marry him!

Frances fought the idea. She was so upset that she became ill for many months. But one day, in the midst of that illness, Frances saw something.

It was like a dream, only more real. A figure was at the foot of her bed, telling her something. It was St. Alexis, and he was telling her that a holy life came from living according to God's will, which might not always be our own.

Frances knew in a flash what this meant. There was nothing wrong with marrying, nothing at all. She could serve God in marriage, and God would make sure she could.

So Frances married and soon had three children. Although her husband was wealthy, Frances tried her best to live simply and use her wealth for the good of the poor. In fact, Frances helped the poor so much that her father-in-law took away her keys to the kitchen and the food storeroom. He didn't want Frances to give away all their food to the poor of Rome!

Frances didn't stop, though. Every time she set foot outside her beautiful home, she was surrounded by the poor and hungry of Rome. How could she say no to anyone when she had so much?

Soon after she married, Frances came to understand that she had a guardian angel who would always be with her to protect and guide her. No one else could tell, but Frances was growing closer to God every day. The eyes of her soul were taking in more and more, and she trusted in her guardian angel's presence.

Frances had much sadness in her life. Two of her children died before she did. During the battles that raged in Rome at different times in her life, her home was destroyed by soldiers and many of her friends were killed.

When terrible things happen to you, what are you able to see? Most of us can't see much at all beyond our own pain and sadness. We can't do much more than put our own lives back together.

But Frances saw more. Listening to God and feeling the presence of her guardian angel, Frances saw what happened as God saw it. She saw that she wasn't the only one suffering. She saw that although she had lost much, she still had enough to help others. Others had nothing, but she still had some things. Others were sick, while she was healthy.

So Frances spent her days and nights helping all the suffering people she saw. She sold all of her beautiful clothes and jewels and gave the money to the poor. She turned her destroyed home into a hospital for the homeless of Rome.

Many people lived in Rome, surrounded by the same kind of suffering. But most of them couldn't see it, and they couldn't see what needed to be done.

St. Frances of Rome did. She wanted to see with God's eyes, so God gave her that gift. She saw God's presence in everything. She saw that God's children were suffering and in need of help. She saw how she could help them.

What would happen if we all opened our eyes as St. Frances did? What would we see? Would we see that there's more to life on God's earth than meets the eye?

St. Frances of Rome saw God's presence everywhere. How would your life be different if you did the same? What would you see that you don't see now?

St. Bernadette Soubirous *1844–1879*

April 16

It's hard to tell the truth sometimes.

But it's especially hard when no one else sees things quite the way you do.

Maybe your friend's gotten into big trouble. You know there's more to the story than what the grown-ups know, but no one will listen to you because they say you're just a kid. They think you're too young to see and understand.

You probably feel very frustrated. It's hard to keep on telling the truth and not back down when other people just aren't seeing the whole picture.

Maybe Saint Bernadette's story will help you out. She was just a young girl who saw something amazing and told the truth about it. Hardly anyone believed her at first, and people even made life difficult for her and her family because of what she said she saw. But Bernadette never backed down, and the truth she told has helped millions of people, even people who live today.

Bernadette's life wasn't easy to begin with. She and her family lived in terrible poverty in a village in France called Lourdes. By the time she was fourteen, Bernadette had been sick so often that she hadn't grown properly. She was the size of a much younger girl. She, her parents, and her younger brothers and sisters all lived in a tiny room at the back of someone else's house, a building that had actually been a prison many years before.

They slept on three beds: one for the parents, one for the boys, and one for the girls. Every night they battled mice and rats. Every morning, they woke up, put their feet on cold stone floors, and dressed in clothes that had been mended more times than anyone could count. Each day they hoped the work they could find would bring them enough bread to live on that day.

Bernadette's life was terribly difficult, but she wasn't a miserable girl. She had a deep, simple faith in God. She didn't mind any of the work she had to do, whether it was helping her mother cook or taking care of her younger brothers and sisters. There was, though, one thing that bothered her. She hadn't been able to attend school very often, and she didn't know how to read. Because of that, she had never learned enough about her faith to be able to receive her first Communion. Bernadette wanted to receive Jesus in the Eucharist, but her days, which were full of hard work, left little time for learning.

Like other girls, Bernadette had many friends. She spent time with them in the countryside, playing and gathering wood for their families' fireplaces and stoves. One cold February day, Bernadette was out with her sister and a friend, doing just that. They wandered along the river until they came to a spot where a large, shallow cave called a grotto had formed in the hilly bank. Bernadette's sister and friend decided to take off their shoes and cross the stream.

Because she was so sickly, Bernadette knew her mother would be angry if she plunged her thin legs into the icy water, so she stayed behind. But after a few minutes, she grew tired of waiting for her companions to return. She took off her stockings and crossed the stream herself.

What happened then was very strange. The bushes that grew out of the grotto walls started blowing around as if they were being blown by a strong wind. Bernadette looked up. High above her in the grotto stood a girl.

The girl was wearing a long white dress with a blue sash and a white veil. Yellow roses were at her feet, and she held a rosary. She nodded at Bernadette and then stretched out her arms.

Bernadette was afraid, of course, but it wasn't the kind of fear that made her want to run away. She stayed where she was and knelt down. She reached into the pocket of her worn-out dress, found her own rosary, and started to pray with the girl. When she finished, the girl disappeared.

Bernadette didn't know who or what she had seen. All she knew was that being there had made her feel happy and peaceful. On their way back to Lourdes, she told her sister and friend what had happened, and soon the whole village knew.

Over the next few weeks, Bernadette returned to the grotto and saw the beautiful girl several times. Each time she went, more people went with her. Although only Bernadette could see the girl in white, when the other villagers prayed with her in the grotto, they felt peaceful and happy too. Those who were sick even felt that God had healed them while they prayed.

During those moments in the grotto, the girl spoke to Bernadette only a few times. She told her that a pure, clear spring flowed under the rocks. She told her that people needed to be sorry for their sins. And near the end, the girl said one more thing: "I am the Immaculate Conception."

Bernadette had no idea what this meant. She repeated it to herself over and over on her way back to the village so she wouldn't forget the strange, long words. When she told her parish priest what the girl had said, he was quite surprised.

The priest knew that what the mysterious girl had said meant that she was Mary, Jesus' mother. The mysterious girl of the grotto had told Bernadette who she was. But it was not very common for people—especially poor little girls who couldn't read—to think of Mary as the "immaculate conception," a phrase that reminds us of how God saved Mary from sin even before she was born.

St. Bernadette Soubirous

When Bernadette told people what the girl had said, it convinced many people that she hadn't made her story up and that what she'd seen really had come from God. Not everyone believed her, though. Bernadette had to tell her story over and over again, sometimes to village and church leaders who weren't very kind to her and her family.

Today, millions of people go to Lourdes every year, to the grotto where Bernadette saw Mary. They go to pray. They go to wash their sick bodies in the spring Mary told Bernadette about. They go to open their hearts to God, as Mary and Bernadette had.

And just think—all of this happened because a young girl named Bernadette told the truth!

St. Bernadette told the truth about what she saw. Why do you think people didn't want to believe her? Have you ever had a difficult time accepting the truth?

Blessed Padre Pio *1887–1968*

September 23

The world we live in is rich and deep.

Most of the time we don't see it, though. We're so busy with school, sports, and other activities that we hardly have time to stop and take even a minute to be quiet and wonder.

Think about what worries you today. Are you anxious about getting your homework finished? Are you concerned about the science test at the end of the week? Are you hoping you'll get to play in the game on Saturday morning?

There's always something. There's your dad telling you that the lawn has to be mowed or the leaves have to be raked. There are those worries about your friends. Why did your best friend act snotty to you today? Why has that boy in the fifth grade decided, for some strange reason, to pick on you every day on the bus?

There's just too much to do, too much to think about.

But sometimes you do stop. Maybe you don't exactly choose to—maybe something happens that makes you stop. Someone you care about dies. On the news you see pictures of other kids your age. Only they live on the other side of the world, and they're thin and hungry. You wonder why.

You're stopped by good things too. You catch a moment of quiet outside at night under a billion stars. Even though you told your mom a long time ago that you don't need to be tucked in anymore, tonight she did it anyway, and deep down, you're really glad. You wonder why.

And sometimes, every once in a while, you know without a doubt that God loves you and forgives you. And you know that your life is a beautiful gift. Everywhere you turn, you see the work of God.

Then, before you know it, it's back to that busy life.

Saints are people who see beneath the busy surface of life. They're people who are such good friends with God that they start to see the world through God's eyes and to love the world with God's heart.

Blessed Padre Pio is one of those holy people. He lived during the twentieth century and passed into heaven only about forty years ago.

Padre Pio was born into a fairly poor family in southern Italy. From the time he was a young boy, he knew that he wanted to be a priest. When he was fifteen years old, he was able to join the Capuchin order, which is a branch of the Franciscan order, the order started by St. Francis of Assisi, who you'll read about on page 205.

During his life, Padre Pio didn't travel much. For almost fifty years, he stayed in the same friary, doing the same work. But soon after he became a priest, something interesting started to happen. People began to hear stories about Padre Pio, stories that interested them very much and gave them hope in God's love. These stories hinted that there was something about Padre Pio that could help people see the power of God's love, even in this busy, distracting world.

So people began to come see Padre Pio.

They attended the masses that he celebrated every morning. Padre Pio didn't take his job of saying Mass for granted. He prepared for each Mass with at least two hours of prayer, and Mass itself would often take up to two hours. Padre Pio prayed through each Mass as if it were his first and only time at the altar. He was in deep union with God.

People also came to Padre Pio for confession. Padre Pio heard confessions for several hours each day, morning and afternoon. People who confessed to Padre Pio told of the great peace they felt after the sacrament. They also told many stories of how, to their great amazement, Padre Pio could read their hearts. He could talk to them about sins they'd forgotten to confess.

That wasn't all. Padre Pio's love of God and his people didn't stop at the church door. One of the most important things Padre Pio gave his time to was a hospital for the poor, called The Home for the Relief of Suffering. He chose the name because he wanted the thousands of people being helped there to feel as if they were being taken care of at home, among family who loved them.

But there's even more to know about Padre Pio.

Have you ever noticed that sometimes, best friends become more alike as time goes by? That's what happened to Padre Pio and his best friend, Jesus.

Early in his life, when he was just a young friar, Padre Pio started noticing pain in his hands and feet. It didn't happen all the time, but it happened enough to make him wonder what was going on.

Then, in 1918, Padre Pio began to share something very important with his best friend. He began to share in Jesus' wounds, the ones Jesus had received on the cross. These wounds are called the stigmata. If a person is closely joined to Jesus and his suffering, the wounds of Jesus actually appear on that person's body. St. Francis of Assisi bore the stigmata, and a few other saints have as well.

You might think of it this way. If someone you love is terribly hurt, you're going to feel that person's pain.

That's what happened to Padre Pio. He saw beneath the world's surface and far above it too. He saw the suffering that sin causes in the world. He saw the pain that sin brought to Jesus on the cross. And because he saw it so clearly with God's heart and God's eyes, he started to feel that pain too.

Blessed Padre Pio

For fifty years—up until he died—Padre Pio bore those wounds of Jesus. He had to wrap his hands and feet in bandages to keep the blood from flowing. Doctors examined him and were amazed. It was obvious that no human person had made these wounds. It was also obvious that, because Padre Pio ate so little every day, losing so much blood should have killed him.

But it didn't, and for fifty years Padre Pio bled with the wounds . of Jesus.

Other stories are told about Padre Pio. It's said that during World War II, some American pilots were flying over the town where Padre Pio's monastery was located. Nazis controlled this town, and the pilots were getting ready to drop bombs on it. When they looked out the window of their airplane, they saw a friar, dressed in his brown robe, floating in the air in front of them. The pilots tried to drop the bombs, but nothing they did would release the bombs. They couldn't bomb the town.

Later, one of the pilots visited the monastery. He'd never been there before. He was introduced to a little friar named Padre Pio. The pilot was amazed. It was the friar he'd seen in the air!

None of this is exactly ordinary, is it? Padre Pio's story shows us that lots of extraordinary things are lurking under all the ordinary busyness of life. We can find them if we just take a moment to look and listen.

Saints are people who've cleared their lives of everything silly and unnecessary. That makes it easier for them to see the world the way it truly is: filled with God's presence and love.

Blessed Padre Pio saw the world through God's eyes. And then he did something else—he gave his eyes, his ears, his soul, and even his body totally over to God.

Do you think he did that so that we could see too?

Blessed Padre Pio shows us that God does extraordinary things when we are open to him. What other stories about God's powerful love do you remember from the Bible and from the lives of other saints? What does this tell you about God?

PART 7

People Who Travel Far from Home

*[Jesus] summoned the Twelve and . . .
sent them to proclaim the kingdom of
God and to heal [the sick].*

Luke 9:1–2

St. Boniface *675–754*

Is your way always the right way?

How do you know?

Are the games you play the absolutely best way to have fun? Do the television shows you watch tell you everything you need to know about the world?

Sometimes we think that the way we live is the best way to live. We get up, go to school, and talk to our friends, who listen to the same music and watch the same movies we do. We go home, eat dinner, and turn on the TV to watch our favorite shows.

We think that's the only way to live. We start to think that everything we hear must be true, because it's what everyone is saying and what everyone believes. Here are some common beliefs:

1. The most important thing in life is having money.

2. The only thing that matters about you is how pretty or handsome you are.

3. You're only worth something if you're cool and have cool things.

We believe these things because there's no one around to tell us anything different. Until a stranger comes to town.

Maybe this stranger is from another country, where people are much poorer than we are in the United States. But the amazing thing is that even though they don't have all the things the commercials tell us we should have to be happy, they're just as happy as we are, if not more so.

Maybe this stranger is a relative or friend who's very rich but very unhappy anyway. Maybe this stranger is a new friend who's disabled. She can't do all the things we think are so important—like being really good at sports. Maybe she doesn't look like a model, never will, and doesn't care. She's happy.

These strangers bring messages, don't they? They bring messages that are true, messages we always knew were true but just couldn't see because we thought our way was the best way.

St. Boniface was a stranger who brought an important message to the places he visited. Like thousands and thousands of Christians, he was a traveler who went to foreign lands to tell people about Jesus and Jesus' love.

Boniface was born in England. It was normal back then for people to be taught by monks, and Boniface received this kind of education. He eventually decided to become a monk himself. After some years working and teaching in the monastery, Boniface took another step and became a priest. He then decided to leave England and do some traveling. He wanted to take the good news of God's love to Germany.

In those days, all of Europe was in constant trouble. Most people were very poor and lived amidst all kinds of dangers. They feared war. They feared wild animals tearing into their crops and homes. They feared diseases taking their babies. They feared changes in the weather—if there was too much or too little rain, their crops would fail, and they would starve.

It was a wild time, and everyone, especially the people in Germany, needed the peace of Jesus. They needed monks and nuns to come into their country to set up schools and places for the sick and homeless.

That's why Boniface went to Germany. He traveled all over the kingdom. He baptized and confirmed grown-ups and children. He helped monks and nuns set up their schools and monasteries. He taught everyone about Jesus' love.

But there was a problem. In every village and town, Boniface met people who didn't want to change. They were used to their old gods. They couldn't believe that there was anything better. They didn't believe Boniface when he said that their gods weren't even real. They thought that their gods had always been there, so of course they were real!

Boniface knew that he had to do something. He knew that he needed to show truth to people in a new way.

Outside of one town stood an enormous oak tree. The people of the town had dedicated the tree to their favorite god, Thor. The people were terrified of Thor. They believed he was the god of thunder and war. They believed that if Thor became unhappy with them, he would send down huge thunderbolts, lightning, and meteors from the sky. He would hurt them and destroy their crops. The people worshiped Thor in great fear.

Boniface called the people to the tree of Thor and told them some shocking news. He was going to destroy the tree.

No one could believe it. This man was going to take an axe to Thor's tree? Wasn't he afraid? Didn't he know that if the tree were destroyed, Thor would erupt in fury and hurt them all?

Boniface picked up his axe. He raised it high and brought it down on the tree trunk with great force. Again, he raised the axe and struck the tree trunk. The tree started to wobble. It made a great creaking sound. Finally, with a mighty thud, it fell to the ground.

The people held their breath. They waited.

Nothing happened. There was no thunder, no lightning, no hail from the sky. A few birds flew around above them, looking for another tree to sit in.

Boniface asked them to look at how the tree had fallen. The pieces of the tree, spread out on the ground, looked like a cross. Boniface explained to them what the cross was and who had hung on that cross out of love for them.

Sometimes it takes a visiting stranger to show us how silly our old ways are. Sometimes we don't see the truth until a stranger comes along to share it with us in a new way.

So next time, let's welcome the traveler. Who knows what good news he or she will bring!

St. Boniface surprised the worshipers of Thor with the news that their god wasn't real. Do people still worship false gods today? Name some, and try to think what St. Boniface would say about those false gods.

St. Peter Claver *1581–1654*

September 9

Imagine that a person in your class is being hurt by teasing.

You know it's wrong to tease a person in a mean way. When you see another person being treated badly, of course you want to help. And there are a lot of ways to help.

You can go to the kids who are being mean and try to get them to stop. You can let the teacher know what's going on so he can do something about it.

And you can go right up to the person who's being teased and help her feel better. You can be a good listener. You can cheer her up by sharing a joke or a funny story. You can try to be her friend.

All of those ways of helping are important. The bad treatment has to stop, and the person who is being hurt needs to be helped. Sometimes we can do both. Sometimes we can only do one. But whenever we see someone hurting, we have to do something.

A few hundred years ago, millions of people were hurting. Their hurt was far more serious than the hurt of being teased. Their pain was terrible and deep.

They were slaves.

When Europeans started bringing slaves to the Americas, a few people saw at once what a terrible evil it was. The slave trade continued for hundreds of years. But here and there, voices rose in protest, and people, mostly Christians, started the slow work of trying to stop the slave trade.

Freedom would be the best help for the slaves. But until freedom came, they needed a different kind of help.

That's the kind of help St. Peter Claver gave. He chose to live in a far-off land so that he could serve people who lived there against their will.

Peter Claver was born in Spain. He studied to be a Jesuit priest. Peter knew, without a doubt, that God wasn't calling him to a safe life in the comforts of home. Peter knew that the New World was the place he needed to be.

So Peter Claver crossed the Atlantic Ocean in a ship that today we'd think was tiny. He had heard that there were people on the other side of the world who needed the love of Jesus. Peter knew that this was where he wanted to be, even though it was far away and he would probably never see Spain again (and he didn't).

Peter lived and studied in the New World for five years before he was ordained a priest. His first assignment as a priest was in a city called Cartagena. Before Fr. Peter arrived at his new home, he thought he would serve the native peoples who lived there. But when he saw the terrible things that were happening in Cartagena, he knew at once that God had something different in mind for him.

Cartagena, located on the far northern tip of South America on the Caribbean Sea, was one of the centers of an evil business: the slave trade.

Cartagena was the first stopping point for many slave ships coming from Africa. Every year, thousands of people were taken there to be sold to rich landowners and mine owners. It was a horrible place.

Seeing the misery and the horror these people faced, Fr. Peter knew what he had to do. He had to, as he said, "be a slave of the slaves forever."

You can't imagine what these slaves had endured on their trip across the ocean. They had been captured and bought in Africa, then packed like animals onto wooden ships. They were given a pint of water a day to drink—that's two cups—and very little food. The slaves were chained to their spots in the boat. Some were chained to the floor and others to narrow shelves that were built into the walls. They had to lie on these shelves day and night.

Of course, there was no medicine, so sick people just got sicker and sometimes died. The trip from Africa to South America took about two months. On some voyages, almost a third of the slaves died, and their bodies were tossed overboard like garbage.

We have to stop and wonder how people can treat other human beings that way. But the slave traders did, and when the boats arrived in Cartagena, the slaves were in awful condition. They were sick and weak, and many of them were covered with sores. They were at the lowest point of misery and unhappiness.

How could Fr. Peter turn away?

Helping these slaves was hard work. The smells that came from the ships were terrible. The diseases that the slaves suffered from sometimes made them look frightening.

But Fr. Peter was focused on one thing. He was focused on Jesus, who told us that when we serve the sick and poor, we serve him. Fr. Peter knew that Jesus would give him the love and strength to help.

In the days before a slave ship arrived, Fr. Peter would go from house to house, begging the townspeople for food to share with the slaves. When a slave ship came in, Fr. Peter would rush out to meet it. He would bring food and fresh water.

The slaves, of course, were very frightened. They had no idea what was about to happen to them. So Fr. Peter brought not only food, but comfort too.

Fr. Peter went down into the hold of the ships to find the sick slaves. He tended their wounds as best he could. He helped the dying in whatever ways he could.

On land, Fr. Peter continued to help. He taught the slaves about Jesus and baptized those who asked to be baptized. He fought for families of slaves to be allowed to stay together. He tried to provide as much comfort as he could.

And Fr. Peter wouldn't let anyone—especially the rich Spanish people who made money off of the evil slave trade—forget that these slaves were human beings and children of God.

Once, a Spanish lady refused to go to Fr. Peter for confession because she didn't want to kneel in the same confessional where slaves had knelt. Fr. Peter told her that that was all right and that he probably wasn't the right priest for fine ladies to confess to anyway.

But the lady wanted to go to Fr. Peter Claver. He was known as a priest of such mercy and love that everyone wanted to go to him for confession. So the wealthy lady decided that she could, indeed, kneel in that confessional.

But she couldn't go to confession quite yet. She would have to wait in line—behind the very slaves she thought so badly of.

For St. Peter Claver, the slaves would always come first.

St. Peter Claver gave his life to the most despised people in his society. Who are the people that our society rejects today? How do Christians continue St. Peter Claver's commitment to serving those people?

St. Francis Xavier *1506–1552*

December 3

What's the longest trip you've ever taken?

When I was a little girl, my parents would drive the family halfway across the country every summer to visit relatives. We drove from Kansas to Maine. For three and a half days, I had to sit quietly in the car, just reading, playing games, or looking out the window. It seemed like forever!

Maybe you've taken long trips too. Maybe you've sat in a plane from morning until night, flying across the country or even across the ocean.

Has your family ever taken a cruise? Even though there's a lot to do on the boat and on the shore, a week is still a long time to spend on a boat, isn't it?

Imagine if you had to be on a boat for six months!

And imagine if that boat was much smaller than a cruise ship, made out of wood and with only sails to make it go. Imagine if several hundred people were traveling on this boat, crowded together, sleeping in hammocks or on the floor, eating dried meat and moldy, crumbly bread, and drinking stale, dirty water.

What a hard journey that would be!

Long ago, before engines were invented, before cars, trains, and ocean liners, that's exactly how people had to travel across the ocean. You'd have to be strong and brave to make that trip.

When Christopher Columbus sailed across the Atlantic Ocean in 1492, he made an amazing discovery. He learned that the world was much bigger than he or anyone else back in Europe had ever thought it was. Columbus and all of the other brave explorers brought amazing news back to Europe. Huge lands lay across the sea, filled with strange animals and plants. Most amazing of all, these lands were filled with people too!

Having heard of these new lands, more people started traveling in tiny ships across the massive ocean to see what was on the other side. Some of them just wanted adventure. Others went because they were filled with greed. They had heard about gold in these new lands and wanted to become rich. They had heard about land and people that would make their own countries more powerful.

But many went across the ocean for a different reason. They had heard about the people in these strange new countries, and they wanted to meet them and give them a great gift: Jesus.

None of the people in the Americas or in Asia had heard of Jesus. They hadn't heard about God and his love. These millions of people needed to hear the good news.

So just as quickly as the conquerors and the merchants set sail, the missionaries also packed their bags and sailed across the rocky, dangerous seas.

St. Francis Xavier was one of the many brave men and women who made that trip, and he's also one of the most admired. That's because Francis Xavier traveled farther than most, planting seeds of Christianity over thousands and thousands of miles.

Francis Xavier was one of the first Jesuits. He was a great friend of St. Ignatius of Loyola (page 211), the founder of that order. He didn't really intend to be a missionary, but when the call came from Ignatius for him to prepare to leave for India, Francis was ready. He sailed from Portugal on his thirty-fifth birthday. He would never see Europe again.

In those days, this is how people got from Europe to India. Their boats sailed into the Atlantic Ocean and then traveled all the way down the west coast of Africa. That part of the journey took five months. Travelers would take a break on an island called Mozambique, and then they would start again, across the rough waters of the Indian Ocean. It took three months to reach India from Mozambique.

Now remember, Francis Xavier didn't have to go on this trip. He could have stayed in Europe, studying and preaching there. But he didn't. Once Francis knew that millions of people in other lands had never heard about God's love, he had to go tell them about it.

The trip was hard, as you can probably imagine. Francis wrote in a letter about one storm that was so bad that the bottom of their ship scraped the sea floor as it crashed up and down on the waves. On such a long journey, with no refrigerators and no ice, food spoiled, and people, even the sailors, got sick. Almost half of them died by the time the ship reached Africa.

I bet that long car trip doesn't seem so bad now.

When Francis arrived in India, he got to work. The earlier Portuguese settlers had brought Christianity with them already. But they had given the Indians a terrible example of the faith. They treated the native people cruelly, and they led sinful lives. Francis had to work hard to fix the harm the cruel Portuguese had done.

Francis tried to reach the Indians any way he could. He walked up and down the streets, ringing a bell. Children would scamper out of their houses and follow him down to the church. There, sitting in the cool shade of the church, Francis would teach the children prayers and songs about Jesus in their own language. He hoped the children would go back and tell their parents about Jesus, and many of them did.

Francis traveled up and down the coast of India. He started forty-five churches there in just a few years. But then Francis heard about a new land, even farther to the east, where Europeans had not yet landed. That land was called Japan.

There was no question in Francis's mind that he had to go. Again he traveled through rough seas. Once in Japan, he walked up the coast through terrible cold, snow, and ice to reach the cities where the Japanese leaders lived. They welcomed him, and Francis was very pleased to discover that the Japanese people were intelligent, educated, and quite eager to discuss religion.

Francis Xavier was the very first person to bring the good news of Jesus to Japan. The communities he started lasted a long time. They even lasted, in secret, through terrible persecution a few years later.

But there was more. The Japanese people talked about still another land: China. Of course Francis had to go there too!

But Francis never made it to China. His boat landed on an island just a few miles off the coast of China, but then Francis fell very ill with a fever. The boats wouldn't wait for him to get well— they sailed off without him.

Left alone on the island with only one friend to help him, Francis spent his last days praying. We're sure that he thanked God for giving him the chance to bring the good news to so many people. We're sure that he prayed for the seeds he had planted to take root and grow.

And as Catholics in Asia know today, they certainly did, thanks to St. Francis Xavier. He was willing to give his life to God's people, who waited for him at the end of many long journeys.

St. Francis Xavier traveled a long way to tell people about Jesus. We may not always have to travel so far. Can you think of people you know who don't know about Jesus' love for them? What do you think is the best way to tell them the good news?

St. Francis Solano *1549–1610*

July 14

Trips can be full of surprises.

Some of them are good surprises—
that's part of the fun of a trip, after all.
Finding a waterfall you didn't know was
there or coming across a neat little
restaurant that serves really great fried
chicken—these are good surprises.

Rain during a picnic lunch and flat tires
are bad ones. That's part of traveling, though. We have to be ready
for all kinds of surprises.

St. Francis Solano was one of the hundreds of missionary
priests, brothers, and sisters who traveled all over the world telling
people about the love of Jesus. Like every one of those other
missionaries, Francis ran into some big surprises, starting with a
shipwreck.

Francis Solano was born in Spain, where he studied with the
Jesuits. He decided to join the Franciscans and was ordained a
Franciscan priest. He served in Spain for many years, but when he was
about forty years old, Francis followed God's call to the New World.

That was in 1589, and believe it or not, missionaries had already
been coming to the Americas for almost a hundred years by then.
Millions of native people were Christians, and thousands of churches
and schools—and even a few universities—had been built.

But there was much more work to do, especially in the jungles
of South America. That's exactly where Francis was headed.

It took many weeks to make that trip in those days, but all went well. Francis's ship crossed the Atlantic Ocean from Spain to Panama. His party then crossed over Panama to the Pacific Ocean, where they caught another boat that would take them to Peru.

One dark night, they came into a storm. The storm rocked the boat from side to side and up and down on the huge waves. The little ship couldn't stand up to the wind and water. It started to break apart.

The ship was filled with all kinds of people: a few missionaries, some adventurers and businessmen from Spain, and lots of slaves. There were lifeboats, but they were reserved for the Spaniards, of course, not the slaves.

So the Spaniards rowed off in the lifeboats. They left a ship that was breaking to pieces, scores of frightened slaves, and one more person: Francis Solano.

Francis could have boarded a lifeboat too. But on the long voyage, Francis had spent most of his time with the slaves, giving them comfort, telling them about Jesus, and even baptizing those who believed. There was no way Francis was going to leave them behind.

So he stayed. He and the slaves huddled together on the ship, which soon began to sink. More than a hundred slaves drowned, and the rest clung to the hull with Francis.

Not long afterward, the hull landed on the shore of an unknown land. Francis and the slaves stayed there, trying to build fires, find food, and stay as healthy as they could. They wondered if they would ever be rescued.

After three days, a ship passed by. The crew saw them stranded on the shore and picked them up. Francis was rescued and taken to safety, but his adventures weren't over yet.

The city Francis was taken to was far away from where he was supposed to be. So Francis started the second part of his journey, this time on foot.

He didn't just walk down the block. He didn't just walk to the next town. Francis walked fourteen hundred miles—as far as it would be if you walked from Florida to Maine.

He walked through ice and snow, high in the Andes Mountains. He walked in the unbearable heat in the valleys below. Carrying the most basic supplies and wearing the brown habit of the Franciscans and only the simplest shoes, Francis walked.

Francis walked that long journey for the same reason any of us travel. He had to reach his destination. Francis's destination was the jungle. The native peoples living in the jungle needed to hear about the love of Jesus. They also needed protection from the Spanish, who wanted to enslave and kill them. During this time, the missionaries were the only people who stood between the native peoples and the cruel Spanish rulers.

Francis eventually arrived at his destination. It was near the edge of fierce jungles, and the people who lived there were suspicious of Francis, as they were of all foreigners. But they soon learned to trust Francis.

Francis made it clear from the start that he loved the native people as his brothers and sisters in Jesus. He helped the poorest among them. He helped the sick. He worked hard to teach them about Jesus.

One of the most wonderful ways that Francis Solano taught the natives was through music. Long ago in Spain, Francis had learned to play the violin. He had even brought a violin with him to America. It had been lost in the shipwreck, but Francis made a new one. It had only two strings, but that was all he needed. The natives were fascinated by his music, and he was able to teach them about God's love through beautiful songs.

Francis had an important task—to bring peace. Not only did he need to protect the native people from the Spanish, but he also had to try to bring peace to warring native tribes. The more time Francis spent with the natives, the more they understood that he wanted the best for them, and the more willing they were to listen.

It's said that once, a war threatened to break out among various tribes. Francis convinced them to gather together. According to the story, almost nine thousand people came that day to listen to him.

He spoke, reminding them of how terrible war was. He asked them to think carefully about all the pain and death a war would bring.

The strange thing about this gathering was that Francis spoke in only one language: the language of the tribe he'd been working with the most closely. The thousands of people who gathered that day spoke many different languages. But they all understood Francis. They laid down their weapons and made peace.

St. Francis Solano certainly encountered many surprises on his trip. He was shipwrecked. He had to walk through vicious weather. He had to make peace among people who spoke many different languages. He even had to make his own violin!

Out of all those surprises came many blessings. That's the way it is on any trip—be it a vacation, a journey to a new home, or even a walk on the pathway of life on earth, which is the biggest trip of all.

Every journey is full of surprises. If we keep thinking about what we'll find when we get to our destination—good things, fun times, and the peace of God's love—we'll make it, no matter what. Especially if we remember that God is with us every step of the way.

St. Francis Solano encountered many surprises on his missionary voyage. Can you think of times when events haven't turned out as you had planned? What did you learn from these surprises?

St. Frances Xavier Cabrini *1850–1917*

November 13

Traveling can be exhausting.

Think of how tired you feel when you reach your destination after a long trip. After you get off the plane or roll out of the car, all you want to do is just take a break and relax.

But all the fuss and worry about luggage and packing and all the miles you put behind you are worth it, especially when you think about your destination. Maybe you're going to see a friend you haven't laid eyes on in a year. Perhaps what's waiting for you is a family reunion with all your cousins, lots of good food, and funny stories.

Or maybe it's a big new city, the mountains, the ocean, or a cabin by a lake. The destination is worth all the trouble, no matter how tired you get.

Let's take a look at the travels of St. Frances Xavier Cabrini. Mother Cabrini, as she's commonly called, spent her whole life traveling. She hardly ever stopped, and travel was a lot harder in her day than it is in ours. But just as it is with you and your trips, Mother Cabrini's destination was worth every mile of discomfort she felt.

There wasn't much in Mother Cabrini's early life to point to such a busy grown-up life. She was born in Italy and had ten brothers and sisters. Her parents were farmers, and their farmland wasn't too far from a river called the Po. Little Frances could look down into the valley and watch the river make its way to the sea. As she looked, perhaps she thought about the stories she heard at home of missionaries. Some say she made boats out of paper, put flowers in them, and set them to sail. The flowers, safe on board, were her missionaries.

By the time Frances was twenty years old, both of her parents had died. So Frances left the farm and started working as a teacher. During this time, Frances grew in faith and maturity. She took religious vows as a sister, worked hard to save a struggling orphanage, and decided to start her own religious order.

Mother Cabrini brought amazing energy to all of these jobs. She was an expert organizer, and it seemed as if everything she touched grew like flowers in a garden, bringing great help to all the poor she served.

By the late 1880s, Mother Cabrini had become interested in a new problem. Hundreds of thousands of Italians had moved to America, seeking a way out of the poverty of their own land. Once in America, most Italians settled together in large cities such as New York, New Orleans, and Chicago. Very few of these immigrants were successful right away. Most lived in worse poverty than they'd endured back in Italy. They were crowded into dirty apartments and lived on scraps. They were barely able to find work. Sad stories traveled back to the home country, right to Mother Cabrini. Something had to be done.

So Mother Cabrini set out on a trip. It would be long, and it would be difficult. But the destination would be worth all the trouble. There were people in need at the other end.

Things didn't start off well. When Mother Cabrini and the sisters traveling with her arrived in New York, they found that there had been a misunderstanding. The archbishop wasn't expecting them. There was no convent ready for them to stay in. They were told by the archbishop's assistant to just get back on the boat and go home!

That, of course, was not going to happen. Since they had no money, the sisters had to stay in a filthy hotel. The sheets and blankets were filled with bugs, and mice and rats ran over their feet.

But soon things began to look up. The next day, the archbishop apologized, and a wealthy woman provided a large house for the sisters. Within four months, Mother Cabrini and her sisters had filled that house with four hundred orphans.

That was only the beginning. Over the next thirty-seven years, Mother Cabrini was constantly on the move, starting schools, orphanages, and hospitals for Italian immigrants and others in need. Let's take a look at just some of the places she went in those uncomfortable boats over rocky seas and in trains that swayed over rough tracks.

Soon after she got things going in New York, Mother Cabrini traveled to Nicaragua to start a girl's school. Then she went up to New Orleans to begin a mission to help Italian immigrants, who faced a lot of discrimination. Then it was back to New York City. After having a dream in which she saw Mary tending to the sick lying in hospital beds, Mother Cabrini started Columbus Hospital.

After she founded the hospital, Mother Cabrini made trips back to Italy to organize more nuns for the work in America. Between these trips, she and some sisters headed back south to Argentina. The sisters went by way of Panama and then Lima, Peru. They made the rest of the journey on train, on mule, and on foot across the Andes Mountains. At one point, while she was carefully making her way across those icy, jagged mountains, Mother Cabrini lost her footing and almost fell into a dark, deep crack in the mountain. But at the last minute she was saved.

Back in the United States, Mother Cabrini traveled constantly, taking her sisters to Chicago, Seattle, and Denver. The sisters impressed the citizens of Denver by tending to the needs of Italian miners. They even went down into the mines to comfort and help the men doing that backbreaking work.

It was in Chicago that Mother Cabrini, at the age of sixty-seven, passed away. She'd begun her work with just a handful of sisters. By the time she died, fifty houses of sisters were teaching, caring for orphans, and running hospitals. Her order had grown to almost a thousand sisters in all. Mother Cabrini was obviously a very holy woman, and the church recognized her holiness by canonizing her in 1946 as the first American citizen to become a saint!

Why did Mother Cabrini do this? Why couldn't she stop traveling?

Mother Cabrini loved Jesus. Jesus traveled through his own land, healing the sick and giving comfort to all who suffered. Jesus said that when we help the poor, the hungry, and the sick, we're really helping him, since he lives in the hearts of all people.

With Jesus as your destination, how could you say no to even one more trip?

Mother Cabrini never got tired of bringing Jesus' peace and love to the suffering. If following Jesus seems too hard sometimes, what can you do to be strong again?

PART 8

People Who Are Strong Leaders

*Your light must shine before others,
that they may see your good deeds
and glorify your heavenly Father.*

Matthew 5:16

St. Helena *250–330*

August 18

"She's a born leader!"

Maybe you know some born leaders. They've been in charge of everything since first grade, right? They love being line leader or class president. They get everyone organized for the class booth at the school carnival.

We all know the born leaders. Maybe you happen to be one. That's great! The rest of us are really glad you love to be in charge—we don't know what we'd do without you!

But you know, not all leaders are that way from the day they are born. Some people have the skills to lead and inspire, but for some reason those talents don't come out until much later in their life.

That's what happened to St. Helena. This strong woman, who lived so long ago, gave Christians a lot of hope and inspiration. But because of hard times and other peoples' cruelty, it wasn't until she was older that she had a chance to share her gifts with the world.

Helena was born into a poor family, late in the third century, in a part of the Roman Empire north of Italy. Her father kept an inn for travelers along a busy highway. Helena worked hard and helped her family from the time she was a little child.

What a busy and interesting life that would be! If you worked with Helena, cooking and cleaning at the inn, you'd have a chance to meet all kinds of people from all over the world. You'd learn a lot about other countries and customs. You might even meet a general or two.

In fact, Helena did just that. One day, when she was about sixteen, a general in the Roman army came to stay at the inn. This general fell in love with Helena, and she fell in love with him. After a few days, it was time for the general to move on, and Helena went with him, as his wife.

What a big change!

Helena soon had a son she named Constantine. She was very happy in this new, exciting life, until one day something happened to change everything. Her husband, the general, was elected to be the emperor of Rome.

Now, you'd think that this would be a good thing for Helena too, but as it turned out, it wasn't. Helena had been just a poor girl before she met the general and married him. In those days, wealthy, powerful men wanted to be married to women from other rich families. This was how they built up even more wealth and power.

So Helena was simply sent away, while her husband, the new emperor, took a new wife.

That could be the end of the story, and it would be a sad one. But it's not.

Years later, Helena's husband died, and her son, Constantine, became emperor. He hadn't forgotten his mother. When he became emperor, he brought Helena back and gave her a title of great honor: "Nobilissima Femina," which means "most noble woman." He also declared her the empress of Rome.

Now that Helena was in an honorable position, she was about to play an important role in history.

For many years, the Roman rulers had persecuted Christians. It was a crime to be a Christian in the Roman Empire. Helena's son, Constantine, changed all that.

Neither Helena nor her family was Christian. But they knew about this strange set of beliefs, and they wondered if it was true.

Constantine got his answer in a famous battle in the year 312. He was about to be defeated by an army that greatly outnumbered his own. At that moment, he had a dream. In the dream, he saw a cross shining in the sky and a symbol for Christ called the Chi-Rho (the first two letters of *Christ* in Greek).

Constantine heard a voice that said to him, "In this sign, you will conquer."

He ordered all of his soldiers to put this sign of Christ on their shields, and sure enough, they won the battle, and Constantine's rule was secure.

This convinced Constantine that Jesus was real and that Christianity was true. He made it legal to be a Christian. The persecutions that had lasted for two hundred years stopped, and Christians could worship without fear.

These events also convinced Helena, Constantine's mother. For the rest of her life, Helena was a strong follower of Jesus. She was a stronger believer than her son, who despite all the help he gave Christianity, did not get baptized until he was about to die.

Helena wasn't like that. She got baptized right away and decided to use her position as the mother of the Roman emperor to help as many people as she could. Helena helped the poor and sick wherever she went. But we especially remember her for a trip she made to the Holy Land when she was almost eighty.

In those days before quick and comfortable travel, Helena had to make her way to the Holy Land on cramped, dangerous boats by sea and in bumpy carriages and on slow, plodding horses by land. But she didn't mind. She was determined to see the places where Jesus had really walked, taught, died, and risen.

As Helena traveled through Palestine, she gave money to the poor. She always wore her plainest clothes to Mass, giving no sign that she was the emperor's mother. When she traveled through a town, the prisoners of that town were pardoned and given another chance to be good.

When she arrived at the holiest sites of all—Bethlehem, where Jesus was born, and Jerusalem, where he was crucified and rose from the dead—Helena did something wonderful.

She ordered that churches be built on those very spots so that people could come and pray in those holy places. She built those churches with her own funds.

Some people say that this story reminds them of Cinderella: a poor girl who, after much hardship, becomes a princess.

That may be so, but there's something different in the story of Helena, isn't there? Helena used the power she was given not to make up for her own unhappy times, but to bring happiness to as many other people as she could.

Maybe St. Helena was a born leader after all!

St. Helena could have done many different things with her leadership skills, but she chose to use them to tell people about God's love. What skills can you use to do the same thing?

St. Leo the Great *c. 400–461*

November 10

What makes a leader strong?

Is it lots of money? a powerful army? a suit of armor and big bodyguards?

Nope. It's none of those things.

Think about the people in your school who are strong leaders. You may even be one of those people yourself. Strong leaders in your class, on your sports team, or in your scout troop aren't strong because of things they own.

They're strong because of who they are inside.

Strong leaders know that what they believe is right. Strong leaders are willing to live by their beliefs, no matter what.

Jesus knew that leaders are a big help. That's why he chose apostles.

We need leaders to help us follow Jesus. We need them to remind us of Jesus' teachings. We need them to inspire us to find the strength to follow Jesus when it's hard to follow him.

Leo the Great was one of those leaders. He came along at a time when Christians needed a lot of help and support.

Leo was a pope during the fifth century. These were scary times for the people of Italy and other places in Europe. For a hundred years, strange tribes from the east had been moving into the Roman Empire. We call them "barbarians," but they were really members of many different tribes with various customs. There were Visigoths, Ostrogoths, Vandals, and Franks. Most frightening of all were the Huns.

The Huns had been trying to invade Europe for years, and by the time Leo became pope, they had come very close. They were almost at the northern border of Italy.

The people of Italy were terrified because they had heard stories about these Huns. The Huns rode on horses, racing through the land in huge armies. It was said that when they ate meat, they ate it only half cooked. That is, when their armies were on the move, they "cooked" meat by placing it between their thighs or on their horses' hot steaming backs for a while.

The Huns were so brutal that they slaughtered whole villages. One Roman told a story of trying to travel through a town that the Huns had attacked. He wrote that he and his party couldn't even enter the town. They had to camp outside. The riverbanks were covered with human bones, and the town smelled so terrible from rotting flesh that they couldn't even go near it without getting sick.

You can imagine how scared the people of Italy were when they heard that the Huns, led by the terrible Attila, were on the other side of the mountains, ready to invade their country.

But there was another, even greater problem. Italy had no leaders.

The Roman emperor no longer lived in Italy—he lived in Constantinople, which is now called Istanbul, Turkey. There had been kings and other rulers in Italy since the emperor left, but none were very strong.

Except the pope.

The pope is, of course, the leader of the Catholic Church. He's also the bishop of the city of Rome. When Italy was at war and the government barely existed, the pope was the strongest leader around. The people looked to the pope and other church leaders for all kinds of help, from helping them find food to organizing schools.

But could a pope—a man without weapons or an army—be any help at all against the fierce Attila the Hun and his thousands of determined soldiers?

Leo was willing to try. He knew there was no other hope.

So Pope Leo set out from Rome and traveled to the mountains in the north. He traveled with only a few others. They went with no weapons and no armor to defend themselves against the arrows and blows of the Huns.

Leo reached the Huns' camp. Attila was waiting for him—he was hard and tough and had the blood of thousands on his hands. What could this priest have to say to him?

The fact is that we don't know exactly what Leo said. Some think he warned Attila of a plague that was threatening Rome. Others say that while Leo was speaking, Attila saw a vision over Leo's head, a figure holding a sword.

Whatever Leo said, it worked. Something about Leo made Attila change his mind. Perhaps he heard the quiet strength in Leo's voice. Perhaps Attila's heart was moved ever so slightly by Leo's deep love for his people, which had inspired him to do this brave thing.

So Attila, to the amazement of all, turned back. He agreed not to invade Italy, and he agreed to negotiate peace with the Roman emperor.

A few years later, Pope Leo did it again. Another tribe—the Vandals—had invaded Rome, and Leo convinced them to not take any lives or burn the city. The Vandals (yes, that's where we get the word *vandalize*!) plundered Rome and took whatever goods they could find. But because of Leo, the buildings and, most important, the peoples' lives were spared.

So, what makes a good leader? Money? Weapons? A fancy, detailed plan of action?

If we want to be leaders, all we have to do is start off with what St. Leo the Great had: faith in God and love for God's people. Armed with that, who knows where our leadership will take us?

St. Leo the Great was a good leader because he knew that he could only lead well if he served God. Think about the skills and talents you have. What happens when you use those skills just for yourself and your own benefit?

St. Wenceslaus *907–929*

September 28

"Good King Wenceslaus looked out
On the Feast of Stephen
When the snow lay round about
Deep and crisp and even . . ."

You've sung that Christmas carol, haven't you? If you have, you know that it tells a story. It's about a wealthy, kind king who looks out his window on the day after Christmas (that's the feast of St. Stephen—December 26) and sees a poor man gathering wood. King Wenceslaus doesn't want to see anyone suffering, especially at Christmastime. So he takes his servant boy, gathers a feast together, and goes on foot, deep into the woods, to surprise the poor man and his family.

It's a wonderful carol and a wonderful story. Did you know that it's about a real person?

It's true. King Wenceslaus really lived. The story that the carol tells may be a legend, but history tells us that what it says about Wenceslaus is true. He was a kind, caring king who was very concerned about the poor. He was a loving follower of Jesus, and his faith helped him be the best kind of leader.

But as we see with so many followers of Jesus—rich or poor, powerful or ordinary—living as Jesus tells us to live can be risky, even deadly. Wenceslaus found this out in a sad way—at the hands of his own brother.

King Wenceslaus was the leader of a part of Europe called Bohemia. His grandmother, who is also a saint—St. Ludmilla—raised him and taught him about Jesus. It was Ludmilla who had

145

helped introduce Christianity to the people of Bohemia, a land located in what we now call Eastern Europe. She was happy to be able to share the good news of Jesus with her own grandson.

You've read stories about ancient kings, queens, and their kingdoms. You know how complicated they can be. The story of Wenceslaus isn't any different.

When Wenceslaus's father died, Wenceslaus's mother, who was not a Christian, became the ruler and tried to discourage Christianity in Bohemia. She hated Christianity so much that she even had her own mother-in-law, Ludmilla, murdered!

Soon after that, Wenceslaus became old enough to claim his role as leader of Bohemia. This took the leadership away from his mother. And since Wenceslaus had been taught so well by his grandmother, he tried to rule over his land as he thought Jesus would want him to.

He tried to bring peace between Christians and pagans. He gave generously to the poor and hungry, knowing that Jesus had said that whenever we help someone in need, we help him. Wenceslaus even translated the Gospel of John into the language of his own people.

One thing Wenceslaus liked to do was travel around his country, visiting villages and especially churches. Once, Wenceslaus traveled to the town where his brother lived. His brother, named Boleslaus, wasn't a Christian. In fact, he had taken their mother's side against Wenceslaus and Christianity. Boleslaus knew that if it weren't for Wenceslaus, he would be the king of Bohemia.

When morning arrived, Wenceslaus went to the town church for his morning prayer. His brother followed close behind. Wenceslaus paused at the door of the church. He knew something was not quite right. His servants had even warned him that something terrible was afoot. But Wenceslaus decided he would trust in God's plan. He looked back at his brother and said, "Brother, you were a good subject to me yesterday."

Bolesaus replied, "And now I intend to be a better one!"

Without another word, Boleslaus drew out his sword and struck his brother. Boleslaus's helpers rushed in and continued to stab and beat King Wenceslaus, leaving him dead on the steps of the church where he had come to pray.

The people whom Wenceslaus had served and loved so well mourned his death and immediately began to honor him as a holy man who taught them a great deal about Jesus.

We don't know whether the old Christmas carol tells the true story about Wenceslaus, but since there's no doubt that Wenceslaus cared for every person in his kingdom, it certainly could be! Perhaps next Christmas when you sing that carol, you'll remember the story about the real King Wenceslaus, the ruler who put Jesus first.

St. Wenceslaus served Jesus in his job as king. When you look around your school, town, and country, do you see leaders acting for themselves or for the good of others? Name some leaders who use their position to help others.

St. John Neumann *1811–1860*

Sometimes life can seem so difficult that we just can't see a way to make it better.

Hard classes in school can really discourage us and even make us feel stupid. There are times when even our family situations get us down, and we wonder if there really is a place in the world where we can be useful and happy.

Those are terrible feelings, aren't they?

If you've ever felt discouraged about your future because of the way your life is now, don't be. One of the lessons that the stories of the saints teach us is that absolutely no one has a perfect life. Every one of the men and women you read about in this book faced hard times, limitations, and suffering. But every one of them was able to do good and even great things anyway.

And more important, every one of them found that God's love lifted them right out of discouragement and gave them more peace and joy than they'd ever known.

If anyone had a right to be discouraged, it was the young man who stood on the deck of a ship on a chilly afternoon in 1836, looking out at America for the very first time.

He shivered in his thin clothes. His head was bare because his hat had been stolen on the journey. He was exhausted from six weeks at sea on this uncomfortable ship. The young man was poor and had purchased the cheapest ticket available to him. A cheap ticket didn't even guarantee him a place to sleep on the boat. He slept wherever he could find a place to lay down his straw mattress and pillow.

So there he stood, a small man—just over five feet tall and not in the best of health—with little money in his pocket, looking out at this land called America, a land that was completely foreign to him. It seems natural that he should be discouraged.

But if we move forward about twenty years, we'll see the same man in a different place. He could walk out the door of his home in the middle of a big city and see the results of all his hard work. He helped build almost a hundred churches, and almost eighty Catholic schools existed because of his work.

Would you say this man was a leader?

This man's name was John Neumann, and he's one of the most amazing bishops we've ever had in the United States. That's why he was one of the first American citizens to be canonized a saint by the Catholic Church.

John was born in Bohemia, now part of the Czech Republic, and studied for the priesthood there. He couldn't be ordained in his own country, though, because they already had enough priests!

So John decided to come to America. He knew that the Catholics there didn't have many priests at all. He knew that the churches in some towns had to wait for weeks at a time for a priest to come celebrate Mass. When John heard about these people in need, he couldn't think of one good reason not to help.

John arrived in America with almost nothing. When he got off the boat, he went straight to the archbishop of New York. The archbishop was expecting him and agreed to ordain John a priest. Soon after he was ordained, John was sent up to the northern part of New York State, around Buffalo.

It was wild country up there in those days. Most people didn't live in towns. They lived on farms or scattered throughout the woods. There was one other priest in the area John was to serve. That meant there were just two priests for hundreds of Catholics that were spread out all over the land. Fr. John had a lot of work to do.

Fortunately, Fr. John was very talented, and his talents were going to come in handy out there in the wilderness. He'd been a very good student. He was especially interested in studying botany (plants) and astronomy (stars). When you're trying to find your way all alone in the woods, it's good to know a lot about both of these things.

It's also useful to know different languages. The people Fr. John served had come from Germany, Ireland, France, and Scotland. It's a good thing that Fr. John knew eight different languages (besides the Greek, Hebrew, and Latin he knew for his religious studies).

For many years, Fr. John served Catholics in the thinly settled lands of New York, Pennsylvania, and Ohio. By 1852, he had done such a wonderful job that he was asked to become the archbishop of Philadelphia, a very important city.

John Neumann was the archbishop of Philadelphia for only eight years before he died suddenly while taking a walk down a downtown street. But during those years he accomplished so much that it would make you tired to even think about it.

In 1852, there were two Catholic schools in the archdiocese of Philadelphia. When Archbishop John Neumann died in 1860, there were one hundred schools. He wrote catechisms, or books of religious instruction, that were very popular. He wrote newspaper articles. He encouraged parishes to pray before Jesus in the Eucharist in a special service called the Forty Hours Devotion. It was a way for everyone to stay focused on Jesus and be strengthened by him.

It was a sad day in Philadelphia when the news spread that Archbishop Neumann had passed away. The Catholics of the city had seen wonderful changes because of his leadership. They had more places to pray, and their children had more schools where they could learn about Jesus.

Who could have imagined that that poor young man who traveled across the ocean to come to this new, strange land would have accomplished so much? Who knew that under those shabby clothes was a heart filled with Jesus' love, ready to share it without thinking twice?

St. John Neumann overcame many obstacles to do great work for Jesus. Think about the parts of your life that discourage you sometimes. What are they? Have you ever prayed and asked God to help you overcome them?

 # PART 9

People Who Tell the Truth

*I am the way and the truth
and the life.*

John 14:6

St. Polycarp *c. 69–c. 155*

February 23

What's the most important thing in your life?

Is it your family? your life? your future? all the stuff you have and want to have?

Would you ever put "truth" on that list?

All of us have a hard time with the truth sometimes. Sometimes it seems that truth just can't be more important than getting what you want or staying out of trouble.

But think for a minute: What would your life be like if truth wasn't important to you or to the people around you? What would it be like if you couldn't trust that your parents were telling you the truth about where they were going to be and what they were going to do? What would it be like if you couldn't trust your teachers to tell you the truth about your assignments? What would it be like if you couldn't trust your friends when they told you they liked you?

Truth is pretty important, isn't it? It's painful to think about what the world would be like if no one cared about telling the truth.

That's why we celebrate saints who put the truth above everything else. We know that they're following Jesus, who told us that he is the way, the truth, and the life. And we know that they're telling us, through the witness of their lives, how important it is to live in a world based on truth, not lies. One of those saints was a frail, elderly man named Polycarp who lived a long time ago.

One bright February day, nineteen centuries ago, thousands of people crowded into a stadium (yes, they had stadiums that long ago!) in a town called Smyrna.

They watched races and games. They ate bread and fruit and drank wine. It was a big party for the whole city in honor of their nation's leader. He was far away in another city, but that didn't stop the crowd from chanting his name in praise. "Caesar! Lord Caesar!" they shouted over and over.

Smyrna was in a land we now call Turkey, but all those centuries ago it was a part of the Roman Empire. So of course, the leader whose name the crowd shouted was the emperor of Rome, Caesar.

They praised Caesar because they thought he was a great man, but also because they believed he was related to their gods. In fact, they thought Caesar was close to being a god himself.

But he wasn't, of course. A growing number of these people's neighbors in Smyrna and people across the empire were refusing to honor Caesar that way. Jewish people had always honored the one true God. Now, another group of people refused to worship anyone but the one true God. These people were called Christians.

Christians bothered the Roman leaders. The Romans worried that if the Christians refused to honor the Roman gods, those gods would get angry and punish the Roman Empire. They wanted everyone in the empire to honor the same leaders and the same gods.

The Roman leaders had an idea. They decided that everyone in the empire would have to show how loyal they were to the emperor. They would make everyone burn incense in front of a statue of him and say, "Lord Caesar." All who did so would prove that they believed the emperor was the most important ruler in their lives.

Christians refused to do this. They knew that no human being could take the place of God. No person, no matter how powerful, could create the world, save us from sin, and give us eternal life.

St. Polycarp

The Roman leaders had an answer for these Christians: torture and death.

So, believe it or not, on days like this February day in Smyrna, when huge crowds gathered to celebrate, the Roman leaders actually made killing Christians a part of the games.

On this day, eleven Christians had already been brought out to fight with lions. Of course, the Christians had been torn to pieces and devoured by the wild beasts. The excited crowd cheered on the bloody show.

But there was still one more Christian left to punish. When the people saw who it was, they broke into the loudest cheers of the day.

His name was Polycarp. He was the leader of all the Christians in the city. He was the bishop of Smyrna. He was eighty-six years old.

Polycarp had been arrested the night before, outside the city in a farmhouse where he had been hiding. The Roman soldiers had tortured a servant until he told them where Polycarp was.

The Roman proconsul—the local leader—silenced the screaming crowd so they could hear his words. He was giving Polycarp one more chance. All Polycarp had to do was take an oath promising that Caesar was his highest leader.

"Swear by the fortune of Caesar," said the proconsul. "Change your mind and say, 'Away with the atheists!'"

An atheist is a person who doesn't believe in a god. When the proconsul said "atheists," he meant the Christians, who didn't believe in the Roman gods or in Caesar as a god. He wanted Polycarp to turn his back on his fellow believers in Jesus.

Polycarp, aged and bent, yet strong because of his faith in God's truth, looked around the stadium. He saw all the faces of those who were calling for his blood. He motioned with his hand.

"Away with the atheists!" he said.

What do you think Polycarp meant when he said those words?

The proconsul gave him another chance. "Take the oath and I shall release you. Curse Christ!"

Polycarp shook his head, slowly but firmly. "Eighty-six years I have served him, and he never did me any wrong. How can I blaspheme my king who saved me?"

The decision was made. Polycarp wouldn't betray Jesus, so he would be thrown to the lions, just as eleven before him had been that very day.

But the lions had already been sent away, so the crowd shouted for Polycarp to be burned to death. Wood was gathered for a fire. Polycarp was stripped and tied to a stake in the middle of the huge pile of wood.

The crowd was in a frenzy. As they cheered for the old bishop's death, the fire was lit. But before his bodily life was ended, Polycarp prayed.

He thanked God for his life and for all of his blessings. He thanked God for giving him the chance to follow so closely in Jesus' footsteps by standing up for God's truth to the point of death. As the fire licked at his flesh, Polycarp gave glory to God and God's truth.

Being faithful to Jesus is very hard sometimes. But is it ever as hard for us as it was for St. Polycarp, who was old and tired but still unafraid of belonging to Jesus, even in the face of death?

St. Polycarp told the truth about Jesus in the face of death. If he had lied, he would have lived. What kind of life would he have had then? What does it feel like to live with what you know is a lie?

St. Thomas Becket *1118–1170*

December 29

What do you do when a friend wants you to lie?

What do you do when telling the truth would hurt your friendship? What's more important: a friendship or the truth?

You can bump into this problem in a lot of ways.

A friend might want you to lie to adults about something that she's done wrong. A friend might not want to invite another friend on a trip, so he asks you to pretend that there isn't anything planned at all. A friend might even try to get you to cheat in school.

What do you do? You might be afraid of losing your friend, but you don't want to do anything wrong, either.

Thomas Becket had this problem too, but it was much more serious.

Almost a thousand years ago, Thomas was close friends with King Henry II of England. Thomas's job was to be the chancellor of the English government. This meant that he was Henry's highest assistant.

Thomas was older than Henry, but that didn't stop them from being great friends. They worked very well together at trying to bring greater peace and order to the people of England.

But Henry and Thomas also had fun together. They talked for hours and enjoyed dinners and parties with the rest of the king's court. They also liked to be outdoors together. From the time he was a child, Thomas had enjoyed being outside. He was a good athlete. He and Henry had wonderful times when they went hunting. They also liked to train hawks and teach the birds how to hunt on command. This sport, called falconry, was very popular in England in those days.

So you can see how close Thomas and Henry were. For years, it seemed that nothing could ever come between them.

But one day something did, and strangely enough, it all started because Henry thought so highly of Thomas.

The main leader of the Catholic Church in England was the archbishop of Canterbury. When the old archbishop died, Henry decided that Thomas would be a wonderful replacement. In those days, kings often worked with the pope to decide who would be the archbishop.

Thomas received the news with dread. It wasn't that he minded serving the church. It was just that he knew his friend, King Henry. He knew that they got along fine most of the time, but when it came to the church, they disagreed. Thomas knew there would be trouble if he became the archbishop. He tried to tell Henry this.

"If you make me archbishop," Thomas said to Henry, "you will regret it. You say you love me now. Well, that love will turn to hatred."

Henry didn't believe Thomas. But he soon saw how right his friend was.

You see, King Henry wanted the government of England to have power over the church. He tried to make a rule that if a bishop wanted to travel outside England, he had to get the king's permission.

King Henry decided that if a bishop died, the government should get control of his land until a new bishop was appointed.

And King Henry decided that if a priest or deacon committed a crime, it was all up to the government to decide how he should be punished. The church could have no say. This was a big change from the way things had been done before.

It's complicated, isn't it? The most important thing to understand is that King Henry wanted the church to do what the government wanted it to do, no matter what.

Thomas, now the leader of all the Christians in England, disagreed. He knew that the government had no right to control the church. He knew that church leaders had to listen to God, not to kings.

Henry had been Thomas's friend for a long time, but Thomas had to tell him he was wrong. It made him sad. He wished things were different. But Thomas knew that the truth was more important than his friendship with Henry.

Now, when you have a disagreement with your friend, things can get difficult and sad. But for Thomas, it was worse. His friend was the king of England. His friend had a lot of power. His friend could make his life very, very hard.

And Henry did. He made Thomas's life so hard that Thomas had to move to France for several years and hide in a monastery. Henry took property away from Thomas's friends and family. Henry tried to get the pope to remove Thomas from his office. The pope refused, and he encouraged Thomas to continue doing the right thing and speaking the truth.

After many years in France, Thomas decided it was time to return to England and face the king, who was really no longer his friend.

On December 1, 1170, Thomas returned. As he rode down the street, crowds cheered, welcoming their beloved archbishop back home. Many people were relieved and happy.

But not King Henry. Trouble and disagreements between them started again right away. One day, Henry became so angry during a meeting with his advisors that he spoke some fateful words: "Who will rid me of this troublesome priest?"

We don't know what Henry meant by these words. But four of the king's knights believed they did. In obedience to their king, they set out on their horses for Canterbury, where Thomas lived.

They arrived on the evening of December 29, just a few days after Christmas. The great cathedral at Canterbury was being prepared for evening services, called vespers. Rumors spread through the town that the knights had come and that they were going to hurt Thomas.

Thomas's friends told him to go to the cathedral, thinking he would surely be safe there. Who would attack someone in a church? Who would attack the archbishop in his very own cathedral?

As Thomas walked across the cool stone floors, four figures emerged from the shadows.

"Where is the traitor, where is the archbishop?" they called.

Thomas answered bravely, "Here I am, no traitor, but a priest of God. I wonder that in such attire you have entered into the church of God. What is it you want with me?" Thomas was asking why these men had come into God's house so heavily armed. The answer came not with words, but with the harsh, bloody work of four swords.

Thomas died, there in Canterbury Cathedral, in front of the altar. Very soon after his death, people started coming to the cathedral to pray and thank God for the powerful life of Thomas Becket, the man who risked everything—even a friendship—for the truth.

St. Thomas Becket faced the difficult choice between truth and friendship. This is a situation that many of us face. Why is it hard to make this choice? What do we risk losing? What do we gain when we choose the truth?

St. Thomas More   *1478–1535*

June 22

There are a lot of ways to tell the truth, aren't there?

We tell the truth when we don't lie. When we're brave and admit that yes, we broke the vase, or no, we didn't study for that test, we're telling the truth.

We also tell the truth when we answer questions completely and honestly. Maybe you studied for that awful test for only five minutes instead of the twenty you should have, and that's why you did badly. If your dad asks you if you studied, and all you say is, "Sure I did," that wouldn't exactly be the whole truth, would it?

So yes, we can tell the truth with our words. We tell the truth when we speak honestly, not intending to trick anyone.

But did you know that we can also tell the truth with actions? Did you know that sometimes we don't have to say a word in order to tell the truth?

St. Thomas More told the truth like that. We remember him because he told the truth not just with words, but in another powerful way—with his actions.

Thomas More lived in England during the reign of King Henry VIII. In fact, Thomas was one of the king's closest advisors. He was a very important part of the English government.

Thomas also had deep faith in God. He was very successful, and he had a wonderful family too. But what brought him the most happiness was his love for God. Thomas was grateful for all the gifts God had given him. He was grateful for his Catholic faith.

But just when life was going the best for Thomas, King Henry made a choice that would change everything.

King Henry VIII was unhappy with his wife, Queen Catherine. He had fallen in love with another woman, named Anne Boleyn, and he wanted to marry her. He wanted the church to release him from his marriage to Catherine.

Now, there are times when the church looks at a marriage and sees terrible problems. For serious reasons, the church will declare that a man and a woman aren't ready to let God's blessings into their marriage. The church will then let the man and woman end their marriage. That's called an annulment, and that's what Henry wanted.

But of course, Henry's reasons weren't serious at all. He was simply unhappy because Catherine had not given him a son and because he had fallen in love with the younger, prettier Anne. Henry even asked the pope to free him from his marriage to Catherine, but the pope said no.

Well, King Henry VIII decided, *if the pope won't do what I want, I'll do the next best thing.*

King Henry declared that he, not the pope, was the head of the Christian church in England. He could then make all the decisions about everything: who the bishops would be, what the churches would look like, and even how the people would pray.

And, of course, whether or not he could marry Anne Boleyn.

So it was done. King Henry VIII cut off the Church of England from the rest of the Catholic Church and declared it his own property. The next step was to make everyone else in England obey this new rule.

Most people did. Almost all of the bishops and priests signed papers declaring the king to be the head of the church. They celebrated the wedding of Henry and Anne and approved of her being crowned the new queen.

But not Thomas More.

Thomas and a few others were horrified. They saw how wrong this was. A king can't be head of a church. They knew that Jesus had made Peter and the apostles the head of the church—not kings, princes, or emperors.

So when it came time to take the oath agreeing with King Henry, Thomas refused.

He was one of the king's most important helpers. He was one of the most famous people in England—in Europe, really. Everyone knew Thomas More as a good man. They knew him as a man who had very strong faith.

Thomas wouldn't take the oath. How could he? He knew that everything Henry was trying to do was wrong. How could he lie? He thought long and hard. He prayed. But in the end, Thomas had to tell the truth. After all, how can you live with yourself when you know you've told an enormous lie?

The king was furious. He needed Thomas's approval so that people would think highly of him and his decision. He put Thomas in prison. He cut him off from his family. Thomas knew that others had been tortured until they agreed with King Henry. The same thing might happen to him.

He stayed strong. He also stayed silent.

Thomas didn't make big speeches about what he believed. He simply stood firm and refused to lie.

So King Henry VIII condemned Thomas to die. Thomas had been his friend and his helper, but that didn't matter. Thomas would be beheaded.

The day came. Thomas was taken from his cell in the Tower of London and was walked through the streets to the place of execution. People crowded the narrow streets and jeered at him. Thin and ill, his hair and beard straggly from his months in prison, Thomas walked steadily. He had spent his last weeks praying, remembering how much Jesus had suffered for us. That had made him strong.

The executioner wore a hood over his face. Thomas forgave him for what he was about to do and even joked with him. Thomas said that since his neck was short, the executioner should be careful.

And after Thomas prayed one more time, he laid his neck on the block and stretched his arms out in front of him. In a second, the deed was done.

Henry ordered Thomas's head to be put on a spike on top of the city walls so that all could see what would happen to a traitor.

But we know the truth, don't we?

We know that St. Thomas More wasn't a traitor at all. To the very end, he was faithful—to God.

St. Thomas More told the truth with his actions. Think about the choices you make every day. Do your actions tell the truth about what you feel and think?

Blessed Titus Brandsma *1881–1942*

July 27

Telling the truth is easy most of the time.

But sometimes, it just isn't.

It's hard to tell the truth when we think it will embarrass us. It's especially hard when we know for certain that telling the truth will bring us pain and even punishment.

Those are the moments when the temptation to lie is the strongest. If a lie will save us from being grounded, why not do it? It's only words, right? It can't really matter that much. Surely being comfortable and safe is more important than a few words.

But is it?

Let's take a look at a man named Fr. Titus Brandsma. Fr. Titus lived in Europe during the twentieth century. For most of his years on earth, he led a busy, happy life, doing the work God had called him to do.

Fr. Titus was a scholar, a teacher, and a writer. He was a member of the Carmelite order. He spent a great deal of time studying and writing about the lives of other Carmelites, such as St. Teresa of Ávila.

Never in the best of health, Fr. Titus worked very hard and spent a lot of time in prayer. He was a popular teacher at the university in the Netherlands where he spent most of his career. Students and other teachers alike thought of Fr. Titus as a good teacher, a good listener, and a trusted friend.

Everything went well for Fr. Titus until the 1930s. Then life began to change for him and for everyone else in Europe. At that time, Adolf Hitler and the Nazi party came to power in Germany.

Quickly, the Nazis spread through Europe, sending their massive armies to frighten countries into giving in to their rule. The Nazis intended to take over all of Europe. They intended to kill all Jewish people. They intended to make belief in God disappear.

In 1940, Germany invaded the Netherlands, the home of Fr. Titus. The Nazis immediately passed laws making it a crime to speak out against them. They ordered all newspapers to print Nazi messages. Even Catholic newspapers, printed by the church for the Catholic people, were supposed to print these messages. The bishops of Holland refused. There was no way they would allow messages of hate to be printed in their own newspapers.

After they made their decision, the bishops gave Fr. Titus an important job. They asked him to travel around the country to all of the Catholic newspapers, explaining the bishops' decision to them and telling them why it was so important to resist the Nazis.

So Fr. Titus began his journey of truth.

He was used to telling the truth. Fr. Titus had been telling the truth about the Nazis for a long time, as a matter of fact. He had told his classes and anyone else who would listen, "That Nazi movement is a black lie. It is pagan." When the Nazis started making laws that punished Jewish people, Fr. Titus spoke out strongly against those terrible laws.

The Nazis had a name for Fr. Titus. They called him "that dangerous little friar."

So of course they wanted to get rid of him.

Fr. Titus didn't get to finish his trip to all the Catholic newspapers. About halfway through his journey, the Nazis arrested him. They gave him a chance to change his mind. They asked him why in the world he would want to work against them.

"As a Catholic, I could have done nothing differently," he answered.

You see, that's exactly what telling the truth is. It's knowing who you are and making the choice to be that person no matter what.

Fr. Titus was taken to several prisons, each worse than the last. At the first prison, he was still able to do some writing, but after that, he was only allowed to do hard physical work. When he could, he gave comfort to the other prisoners. He shared his food. He listened to their confessions. He blessed them and gave them courage to endure beatings and torture, even if just for one more day.

Finally, Fr. Titus was sent to Dachau. Dachau was a concentration camp where hundreds of thousands of prisoners, mostly Jewish people, died. It was pure misery. Fr. Titus was put in a barrack that was just for people like him. He was in the company of more than sixteen hundred other priests and ministers.

Fr. Titus had never been very healthy, and it was a miracle that he had survived for as long as he did. Even as he got sicker and sicker in Dachau, he tried as long as he could to avoid the camp hospital. He knew the truth about this hospital. It was a place where Nazi doctors did horrible medical experiments on patients, adults and children alike.

But soon, it couldn't be avoided. Fr. Titus, near death already, was taken to the Dachau hospital. He was too ill to be used for the experiments, so it was decided that he would just die. One day in July, a nurse injected Fr. Titus with a deadly poison. Before he died, Fr. Titus gave that same nurse his rosary.

Fr. Titus Brandsma didn't have to tell the truth. He knew that if he did, he would be punished and would probably die.

But Fr. Titus made a choice. He made a choice to love God, which means that he chose to love truth.

Which do you think is a better world to live in: one where people love truth or one where people don't care?

Blessed Titus Brandsma knew that truthful words are important. Are there times when you think telling a lie isn't such a big deal? When are those times, and why do you feel that way?

 # PART 10

SAINTS ARE

People Who Help Us Understand God

*How can I [understand], unless
someone instructs me?*

Acts of the Apostles 8:31

St. Augustine of Hippo *354–430*

August 28

Do you remember when your soccer team made it to the championships?

It was all you could think about for days. You imagined how great it would feel to win. You thought about how cool it would be to see your team's picture in the newspaper. You just knew that winning the championship would make you happier than you'd ever been before.

And just as you'd dreamed, it all happened: the win, the trophy, the pizza party afterward, and even the newspaper photograph with your name in the caption.

Months later, did it still seem so important?

What about that ribbon you won for your science project last year? Do you even know where it is now?

We won't even talk about those Christmas presents you begged and pleaded for last year, those toys and games you knew you couldn't live without. Isn't it odd how you've practically forgotten about almost every one of those things you swore would be all you needed to be happy? Don't you wonder if there's anything out there that will bring you happiness today, tomorrow, and forever?

Augustine of Hippo was a young man who puzzled over that very question. Just like you, he enjoyed doing different things and he took pride in his accomplishments. All of his paths brought him happiness and pride, but none of it lasted. Augustine's heart yearned for a happiness he could depend on.

Augustine lived in North Africa and Italy during the fourth and fifth centuries. You've read a little about his life in the story of Monica, his mother (page 19). You know that her prayers were important in helping Augustine discover real happiness. Now it's time to tell the story of exactly what happened to Augustine.

He was such a smart boy, that Augustine. He loved life and everything about it. He loved to learn, he loved to play, and he loved to spend time with his friends.

All of these things gave him joy and pride, but Augustine started noticing something about those good times: they always ended. Friends moved away or even died. After a while, his successful career began to seem almost useless.

Augustine found happiness with the woman he lived with. They had a child and named him Adeodatus, which in Latin means "gift of God." So Augustine knew that love and children were a good part of life. Even so, he sometimes wondered if that kind of happiness was distracting him from something even deeper that would last beyond life changes and even death.

Augustine also found happiness in his beliefs. The trouble was that Augustine didn't believe in one thing for very long. Once, he spent some time believing in a certain religion, one that believed in two gods, only to find out later that it was false.

By the time Augustine was in his early thirties, he had tried everything he could to find happiness. Nothing had worked. Augustine had no peace in his heart.

As you know, Augustine had been raised a Christian by Monica, but he wasn't baptized. He knew a little bit about Christianity. Now he began to actually study it, and he discovered that he didn't know as much about it as he thought he did.

What he learned was something simple: Jesus wasn't a character in a story. He had really lived, died, and risen from the dead. He had spoken the truth about God and the world. And Jesus continued to live, teach, and love the world through his church.

Augustine knew now that putting Jesus—who lives and loves forever without changing—at the center of his heart would bring him that happiness he'd been looking for. But he was afraid.

Augustine knew that if he gave his life to Jesus, his life would be very different. He'd have to give up many of the things that gave him momentary happiness. Some of these things were clearly wrong, but other things were simply a waste of the time he could be devoting to God.

This was so hard for Augustine. You can imagine how he felt. Augustine had to turn his back on things he could see and touch. The rest of his life's happiness would depend on something he couldn't see.

One afternoon, he was in a friend's garden, thinking about all this. He wanted to belong to Jesus, but he didn't think he was strong enough to give up all the fun times and worldly success he was used to. He was so upset that he could hardly think.

Suddenly, he heard voices. They were children's voices, chanting as if they were playing a game. This is what they were saying in Latin: "Tolle et lege! Tolle et lege!"

This means, "Pick up and read! Pick up and read!"

Augustine looked around. An open Bible sat on a nearby table. He picked it up and read the very first passage his eyes rested on. It was from Paul's letter to the Romans. The verses said that if we wear the power of Christ like a suit of armor, we'll be strong enough to do anything.

In a flash, Augustine understood. He understood that he couldn't take this great big step on his own. But if he turned to Jesus as his Lord and friend and asked him for strength, that would be enough to help him take that first step.

Augustine did just that. He found the kind of peace and joy that nothing else in life had ever given him. He spent the rest of his life serving God, who'd given him such a lasting love. Augustine became a priest and a bishop. He defended Christianity against unbelievers. He was a wonderful teacher. After sixteen centuries, his books are still popular. They have been translated into many languages and have been read by people all over the world.

St. Augustine's long, hard road to a peaceful heart teaches us something important yet simple about God. God is the one who's there for us no matter what.

Other people are going to disappoint us. What we think is fun one minute might really hurt us the next minute.

But God won't disappoint us. He won't bore us, and if we listen to him as he speaks to our hearts, he'll help us be our best selves, the people he created us to be. That, in the end, is what brings us peace now and forever.

God is love. In God we find a place where happiness is always alive and never fades away. He made us to be with him forever. This is exactly what St. Augustine meant when he said: "Our hearts are restless till they rest in you, O Lord."

St. Augustine helps us understand that God's love is all we need to be happy. Name some things that you thought would bring you happiness but didn't. Why do you think those things lost their power to bring you happiness?

St. Jerome *c. 341–c. 420*

September 30

Do you ever have questions about God?

Where do you look for the answers? Your parents and grandparents know a lot. Your religion teacher can certainly help you out. If you listen carefully at Mass, you will surely learn quite a bit.

And then there's the Bible.

Of course! Where would we be without the Bible?

You know that the Bible is the first place to look if you want to understand more about God and his love. But did you ever wonder how we got the Bible?

You know how it began. Over hundreds of years the Holy Spirit inspired people to write down what God revealed to them.

You know the end too. You know that the Bible sitting on the table beside your bed was printed and bound by machines and sold in a store to someone who cared enough to give it to you.

But what about all those years in between? Don't you ever wonder how the Bible actually got from there to here?

People, that's how. Thousands and thousands of people cared enough about God's word to pass it on, first by telling stories, then by writing them down, then by copying them—again and again.

The printing press wasn't invented until the 1400s. Before that, the only way books could be made was by writing them out by hand.

Can you imagine writing out the whole Bible by hand? The fact that thousands of people spent their lives copying the stories of the Bible is something to be grateful for, isn't it? Most of these people were monks and nuns, and they copied the Bible so that future generations—that's you and me—could learn about Jesus.

And what about language? How did the books of the Bible get from the Greek and Hebrew in which they were written to a language you and I can understand?

Well, people spent their lives translating the Scriptures into different languages. And St. Jerome is one of the most important people we should thank for giving us the Bible in a language we can understand.

To get to know St. Jerome, we have to go back a few years—a little more than fifteen hundred. We also have to cross the ocean, not to the great universities of Europe or to the enormous libraries of Egypt, but to someplace a lot simpler and more surprising: a cave.

Yes, a cave. A large cave in the hills outside of Bethlehem. The flames of candles and oil lamps dance in the darkness, letting us see what's going on.

Ancient books and hundreds of sheets of thick paper are piled on wooden tables and shelves. A man with a flowing white beard sits at a desk, studying and thinking. He writes with energy and speed. The man stops only to pray, to talk with visitors, and to eat just a bit, now and then, here and there.

Meet Jerome. He's translating the Bible—the whole thing.

He doesn't have a computer. He doesn't have electric lights. He doesn't have a copy machine. All he has is his own hand and the strength God gives him to work at this amazing task.

St. Jerome

In Jerome's time, back in the fourth century, Latin was becoming the most important language for the church. Greek was important too, but more and more church leaders and teachers were using Latin.

But the Bible wasn't written in Latin. The Old Testament was mostly in Hebrew, and the New Testament was in Greek. Someone had to translate those words into Latin so that the good news could be spread far and wide. Jerome agreed to take on the job.

Jerome had been born in Italy, but he moved to Bethlehem with friends. He knew that being closer to the places where Moses, David, and Jesus had lived and walked would help him do a better job. Jerome didn't know Hebrew, so he worked with a rabbi to learn it. He needed a lot of help with all of the copying, so the friends who lived in his monastery helped out.

Two of his closest friends and greatest helpers were women. Their names were Paula and Eustochium. Jerome was very grateful for their help. When we think about how blessed we are to have the Bible, we should think about their hard work too.

There outside of Bethlehem, so many centuries ago, Jerome worked in a cave, in the heat of summer and in the chill of winter. He read slowly, maybe about Abraham one day and about Solomon the next, making sure he understood exactly what the Hebrew words meant. He thought carefully about which Latin words meant the same thing. Then he used his pen—probably a thin, carved bone he could dip in ink—to scratch out God's word on sheets of paper made from either animal skin or the papyrus plant.

Jerome worked all day and into the night, until the oil in his lamp ran dry. And then he slept for a few hours, woke up, refilled his lamp, and began again.

Jerome knew the Bible was important enough to spend his whole life copying and translating it. That might mean it's important enough to actually read, don't you think?

St. Jerome gave his life to passing on God's word in the Bible. Do you read the Bible? If you don't, where do you think would be a good place to start?

St. Patrick *c. 389–461*

March 17

Some teachers have really small classes.

When your dad taught you how to cook, he had a class of exactly one. When your scout leader showed your troop how to set up camp and build a fire, her class was a little bigger, but still pretty small.

How many students are in your class at school? Thirty or so? Still bigger, but not huge.

Try this one.

How do you teach a class that's as big as a whole country? How do you teach a whole country about God?

What a big job that would be. It's a job that would seem scary and even impossible to most of us.

But it wasn't to St. Patrick, whose classroom was the whole country of Ireland and whose lesson was the good news of Jesus Christ.

Before television, before computers and telephones, before cars, electricity, the printing press, or anything else that makes communication fast and easy, St. Patrick taught the entire country of Ireland about Jesus. It took him only about twenty years.

How in the world did he do it? Well, it was only possible because he depended totally on God.

But letting God give him strength and direction didn't always come naturally to St. Patrick. That was a lesson he had to learn himself. And he didn't get to learn it from understanding, gentle teachers in a comfortable classroom. He learned it from a band of thieving, roving pirates.

Although we think of Ireland when we talk about St. Patrick, he wasn't actually born in Ireland. He was born in Britain, perhaps even in Scotland. His father was a deacon, and his grandfather had been a priest. But Patrick didn't think too much about God.

We don't really know why this was. He probably thought he didn't need God. He probably thought other things could bring him as much happiness as God could. God just wasn't on Patrick's mind as he roamed the fields of his homeland, tending animals and learning how to be a man.

But his happy, carefree life ended one day when crowds of strangers appeared on the horizon. They looked dangerous and frightening, and they were. They were pirates and thieves, on their way to capture slaves to take back to Ireland.

Patrick was one of those hundreds of captives. He was snatched from his family and his home. He was taken from all of his future hopes and dreams. Patrick was thrown on a ship, bound in chains, and taken over the sea to Ireland. He was sixteen years old.

For six years, Patrick was a slave in Ireland. He was put to work watching sheep and cattle. Patrick had just enough food to live on, and when he wasn't working, he tried to rest in tiny huts that were damp and cold.

But something strange and wonderful happened in Ireland. All alone, frightened for his life, and among people who worshiped trees and stones, Patrick opened his heart to God.

St. Patrick

That happens to a lot of us, doesn't it? When everything's going great, we don't have any time for God. But then something awful and painful happens, and there we are, back at God's feet.

During those years, Patrick started to pray. He thought about God all the time, and it gave him peace of mind. He knew that no matter how much he was suffering, God loved him.

Eventually, Patrick escaped from slavery and traveled to France, which in those days was called Gaul. We're not sure exactly how much time Patrick spent in Gaul. But it was enough time for him to draw closer to God as he prayed and studied in a monastery.

One night, deep in a dreamy vision, Patrick heard voices. He heard many voices, joined together, pleading with him.

"Come back," the voices cried, "come back and walk once more among us."

Patrick knew it was the Irish people calling him.

Strengthened by the courage that only God can give, Patrick went back. He returned to the very people who had stolen him from his family, worked him mercilessly as a slave, and knew little, if anything, about the love of the true God.

Before he left Gaul, Patrick was made the bishop of Ireland. He then traveled across the sea to teach Ireland about Jesus Christ.

It wasn't easy. The people of Ireland practiced pagan religions. They worshiped nature, and they practiced magic. They feared the spirits they believed lived in the woods. The Irish people believed they could bring evil spirits down on those they wanted to harm.

Patrick had a big job ahead of him. He had to show a country full of students that there was no point in worshiping nature. Trees can't forgive your sins or teach you how to love. The sun, as powerful as it is, could not have created the world.

Patrick explained things using simple examples that people could easily understand. For example, he used the three-leaf clover to show people how there could be three persons in one God.

Patrick preached to huge crowds and small villages. He preached to kings and princes. He preached in the open air, and he preached in huts. Patrick never stopped preaching, and he never stopped teaching. He couldn't stop—the whole country of Ireland was his classroom, and he couldn't afford to miss even one student!

Soon, Patrick had help. Men became priests and monks. Women became nuns. Wherever they lived, those monks and nuns settled in monasteries and set up schools. More students were being reached every day.

But, of course, the greatest help Patrick had was from God.

When he was young, Patrick had forgotten God, but that would never happen again. He knew that God supported him in every step he took. God gave Patrick the courage to speak, even when Patrick was in danger of being hurt by pagan priests who didn't want to lose their power over the people.

Patrick's most famous prayer shows us how close he was to God. It's called "St. Patrick's Breastplate." A breastplate is the piece of armor that protects a soldier's heart from harm.

Christ with me, Christ before me,
Christ behind me, Christ within me,
Christ beneath me, Christ above me,
Christ at my right, Christ at my left.

St. Patrick's courage and faith helped him return to a land filled with the same people who had tried to hurt him before. St. Patrick's heart was so filled with the love of Jesus that he was ready to risk everything to help the people of Ireland understand God and see how God's love could transform every corner of their lives.

St. Patrick

St. Patrick taught the people of Ireland about God's love. Today, the Irish people are still grateful for his work and sacrifice. Think about your good teachers. What are the best lessons they taught you? Say a prayer of thanks for these teachers.

St. Thomas Aquinas *1225–1274*

January 28

Thomas was a big, quiet boy.

Perhaps you know someone like him—someone who sits in class, day after day, saying little or nothing, listening to the teacher sometimes or staring out the window.

And then one day, this quiet person whom no one has ever noticed says something amazingly smart. Maybe it's an answer to a question. Maybe it's an explanation of a point the teacher is having trouble explaining.

Whatever this person says, when he speaks out of the blue, everyone in the class turns around. They notice for the first time that this boy might just be something special.

That's what happened to Thomas. His classroom was different from yours. There weren't any desks, books, or notebooks. The students crowded together on benches and tried to listen to what the teacher was telling them, nudging each other and giving each other little kicks, hoping that they wouldn't get caught.

And then, Thomas spoke. All of a sudden, out of nowhere, he asked a question: "What is God?"

Thomas Aquinas would spend the rest of his life answering that question, the most important question anyone can ask.

Thomas Aquinas was brilliant. Smart people can use their minds in any way they want. They can invent new things. They can write great novels. They can build successful companies.

But for Thomas, who loved God above everything else, there was only one way to use his brilliance: to understand God and explain God to the rest of us.

"What is God?" Thomas's answers to this question, given to us in huge volumes, are some of the most important answers anyone in our church has ever given to that question.

But if Thomas's family had gotten their way, none of that great thinking or writing would have happened at all. You're not going to believe what Thomas had to go through just to be able to spend his days thinking and praying the way God wanted him to!

If you ever feel picked on by your older brothers or sisters, think about Thomas Aquinas. He had seven older brothers, and not one of them understood him. Neither did his parents.

His family wasn't the richest in Italy, but they weren't poor, either. Thomas's father was a fairly wealthy nobleman who was happy to raise his rowdy group of sons to go out, fight wars, and bring more wealth to the family.

But early on, it was clear that Thomas was different. He was quiet and not very athletic. He liked to study, pray, and be alone.

That was okay at first. His father didn't mind because he had all those other sons to carry on his worldly ways. If Thomas wanted, he could join a monastery—in fact, he could join St. Benedict's monastery, high up on top of Monte Cassino.

After many years with the Benedictines and some time at the University of Naples, Thomas decided that God was calling him to the Benedictine life. Then, during his studies, he met some members of a new religious order: the Dominicans. The Dominicans were quite different from the Benedictines, who had become rather rich and comfortable (certainly not what St. Benedict had planned when he started the order).

The Dominicans, whose order had been founded by St. Dominic (see page 81) twenty years before, weren't settled like monks. They weren't even monks. They were called "friars" (which means "brothers"), and their call was to wander, beg, study, and teach.

This is what Thomas wanted? This is what Thomas—son of Count Aquino, who was known and respected throughout Italy for his fine life and family of brave, swaggering sons—wanted to do with his life?

Count Aquino didn't think so.

Thomas had already joined the Dominicans when he heard of his family's outrage. His mother came to ask him to change his mind. He said no. Just to be safe, the Dominican friars decided to move Thomas to Paris, where he could study at the University of Paris and be farther away from his family.

It was a good idea, but it didn't exactly work.

Thomas's mother had already sent word to his brothers. Just past Rome, they lay in hiding by the road, waiting for Thomas and his new brothers to pass.

Then they attacked. They wrestled their large brother to the ground. They ripped his white and black robes. Finally, they put him on a horse and took him away.

They took Thomas back home to the family castle. They locked their brother up in a high tower and waited for him to change his mind. Thomas stayed in that tower for two years.

Can you imagine?

It's hard to understand why Thomas's family did this to him. But you've seen it happen before. Many saints had to overcome their families in order to follow God's call. St. Francis of Assisi and St. Catherine of Siena had to. St. Wenceslaus was murdered by his own brother because of his faith!

Sometimes families can't understand the strange things God wants us to do. Thomas's family certainly didn't. His decision to use his talents for God in this special way was just too much. They thought it would actually bring shame on their family.

It got so bad that Thomas's brothers even sent a beautifully dressed woman to tempt him away from focusing on God. Thomas had been patient until then, but this was too much. He picked up a poker that was resting in the fire, and he waved it angrily in the air. Of course, the woman ran for her life, and Thomas, in a rage, thrust the hot poker right through the wooden door of his room in the tower.

That was enough to show Thomas's family that he was serious about his decision. They finally gave in and let Thomas rejoin the Dominicans and move on to Paris.

Happy and at peace, Thomas went.

He was still quiet, so quiet, in fact, that his fellow students at the university called him "the big dumb ox." He never said a word during classroom discussions, but when other students came to him for help with their studies, they were amazed at Thomas's deep understanding of philosophy and faith.

Thomas led a busy, peaceful life after that. He became well known throughout Europe as a brilliant teacher and writer. The pope himself called Thomas in to help explain hard teachings.

But just as important, his fellow Dominicans knew Thomas as a man who loved God. His mistreatment by his family didn't leave him bitter or angry. Thomas knew that just as God forgives us, we're called to forgive others.

So Thomas loved, prayed, studied, and taught. His family had feared that Thomas would bring shame to their family. They wanted him to be like them, living for riches, glory, and fame.

But Thomas followed God's call in his conscience.

And who are we talking about today—the brothers who looked for fame, or the one who avoided it? Who has given more to the world—the brothers who used their talents only for themselves, or the one who used his gifts to serve God?

St. Thomas Aquinas followed God's call even though his family didn't support him. Why do you think that family members sometimes don't support each other? Think of the gifts the members of your family have and how you can encourage them.

St. Edith Stein *1891–1942*

August 9

Why do you go to school?

Do you go because your parents make you? because you like to be with your friends? Do you go to school to learn, maybe? about math, science, history, and all that stuff?

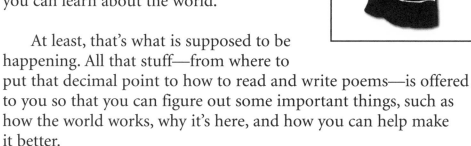

You go to school so that bit by tiny bit you can learn about the world.

At least, that's what is supposed to be happening. All that stuff—from where to put that decimal point to how to read and write poems—is offered to you so that you can figure out some important things, such as how the world works, why it's here, and how you can help make it better.

Everything you learn is a sort of building block. When you learn, you're building your life. Some blocks are big, some are tiny, and some don't seem to fit at all into what you're building.

At some point—maybe soon, maybe not for a few more grades—you'll find a subject that gets you excited and that you're really good at. Whatever it is—art, science, literature, or computers—you'll have found the solid building block that will help you make a great big building, one you can spend the rest of your life in.

When you find this building block, you'll have found something else as well. You'll have found your own little corner of truth. But there's no way that any one person can understand all of what's true and real. Each of us, with our special interests and talents, can understand a little part of it, and together we can build a world that's an expression of the truth of God's creation and will.

All saints are interested in truth. What makes them saints is that when they find it, they won't let go, no matter what. Once they find the most important truth of all—God and his love—they never want to go back to lies or even half-truths again.

Edith Stein was one of those saints.

Edith was born in Poland, which at the time was a part of Germany. Her father died when she was only two years old. This left Edith's mother to care for her large family and the family's lumber business by herself.

She did it, though, and she did a wonderful job because she was a very strong woman. That's the kind of woman Edith Stein grew up to be—strong, just like her mom.

Edith's family was Jewish, but when she was a teenager, Edith turned her back on her faith. She was quite smart, and she thought she was too smart to believe in God. She wanted to find truth, but she couldn't imagine that God had anything to do with it.

So Edith went to school and studied hard. In college, she studied philosophy, which was a rather unusual subject for a woman to study in those days.

That didn't matter. Edith was strong. She didn't care what other people thought. She was after truth, and that's what philosophy is all about. Philosophers ask questions such as "What's real?" "How do we know anything?" and "What's the meaning of life?"

Edith was brilliant. Many agree that no other philosophy student in Germany at that time was as smart as she was. She wrote papers and books. She became a teacher. She went about her life, busily teaching and writing.

But even then, Edith had not quite found what she was looking for. She could talk to you about what it means to be a person. She could explore all kinds of other deep subjects. But something was missing from Edith's life.

One day, one of Edith's friends died. Edith dreaded going to visit her friend's wife. She was afraid that the wife would be too sad and that Edith wouldn't know what to say to help her.

But that's not what happened. The young widow was indeed sad, but she wasn't angry or depressed. She told Edith, very simply, that she knew her husband was with Jesus now and that someday she would follow him. She knew this was true, and that truth gave her peace and hope.

This was a strange thing for Edith to hear. She had studied truth for many years, but she didn't think that any of those ideas, all by themselves, could bring her peace if someone she loved died.

Edith started thinking. She started reading other books. One night, she sat up all night reading about St. Teresa of Ávila. (St. Teresa's story is on page 85.) She read about St. Teresa's strength, her happiness, and her deep love of God. In the morning, Edith set the book down and thought, *This is true.*

So, after more study and a lot of prayer, Edith Stein became a Catholic. She knew that God was real and that he'd come to earth in Jesus. She knew this was true.

Edith kept studying. She still wrote about philosophy, but it was different now. Now she saw the whole truth about the world, and she was happy to live in that truth.

Eventually, Edith made another decision. She decided to become a nun—a Carmelite, the same kind of sister St. Teresa was. In one way, it was an easy decision, but it was also hard. Edith's mother had been very upset when Edith became a Catholic. Edith's joining a convent was worse.

But after saying good-bye to her mother with tears and love, Edith went where truth was leading her. She went to the place where she could spend her days and nights praying, thinking, and writing about God's love. In the convent, Edith's name became Teresa Benedicta of the Cross.

There is more to the story of Edith Stein. She spent her life looking for truth, but in the end it was the evil of lies that took her life.

The lies were Nazi lies. The Nazis said that Jewish people should be destroyed. Because Edith was from a Jewish family, she was arrested and imprisoned in a concentration camp.

Edith, St. Teresa Benedicta of the Cross, died bravely in that concentration camp. She was filled with love and compassion for her fellow prisoners to the very end.

Through all her searching, St. Teresa had found the truth of Christ's love. We know that, through faith, the truth set her free in the end.

St. Teresa Benedicta of the Cross was devoted to the truth. Look around your world. Think of one person you know who is dedicated to truth. Who is that person and how do they share their dedication with others?

 # PART 11

SAINTS ARE

People Who Change Their Lives for God

*Put on the new self,
created in God's way in righteousness
and holiness of truth.*

Ephesians 4:24

St. Ambrose *340–397*

December 7

Have you ever been chosen to do something you weren't sure you could do?

Maybe your softball coach thought you'd be a great pitcher, but you didn't know if you agreed. Or maybe a teacher gave you the great news that she had given you a part in the play—even though you hadn't even tried out!

Maybe you felt nervous about doing this thing that you weren't sure you could do. But what did your coach or your teacher tell you? What did your mom tell you when she left you to take care of your baby brother for the first time by yourself?

"You can do it. I know you can. I've got faith in you!"

Something just like that happened hundreds of years ago to a man named Ambrose. Ambrose was asked to be a bishop—and he hadn't even been baptized yet!

Ambrose lived in a city called Milan, which is in the northern part of Italy. In Ambrose's time, Italy was part of the Roman Empire, which covered most of Europe. An emperor ruled the whole empire, but because the empire was so big, other people were put in charge of smaller parts of it. The emperor put Ambrose in charge of Milan. Ambrose was called a prefect.

As the prefect of Milan, Ambrose had to make sure that the city was clean and that the people treated each other well. Sometimes that was a problem. People broke laws and they hurt others. But Ambrose treated everyone fairly and helped keep peace in the city.

There was also a bishop in Milan. He was in charge of the Christian church in the city, but the people did not like him. He taught something about Jesus that was wrong. He believed that Jesus was not really God, and he punished people who did not agree with him. The people of Milan were quite unhappy with their bishop.

In 374, the bishop died. In those days, when a bishop died, the people of the city he served elected someone to replace him. The emperor was afraid that there would be trouble—even fights—over who the next bishop should be. So he asked Ambrose to pay special attention during the election and keep the peace.

The people of Milan went to their main church—called a basilica—to elect a new bishop. They were crowded inside, arguing and shouting about who the new bishop should be. Ambrose came to the church and started talking to the people there. As he was reminding the people to be peaceful in their election, a cry came from somewhere in the crowd.

"Ambrose for bishop!"

Ambrose was surprised, but he tried to keep on talking. Soon everyone in the crowd was shouting the same thing: "Ambrose for bishop!"

Before he knew it, Ambrose had been elected the new bishop of Milan!

The people had decided that they wanted Ambrose to be the leader of their church because he had been such a good leader of the city. But there was one problem. Ambrose hadn't been baptized yet.

His mother was a Christian and had raised Ambrose in a Christian home. Ambrose believed in Jesus, but at that time, people did not usually get baptized until they were adults. Ambrose was still what we call a catechumen, not a full member of the Christian church. But he must have been quite a great man if the people thought he was the right choice for bishop!

Ambrose was not happy at first about being elected bishop. He even hid from the people for several days, hoping they would give up and pick someone else. But they wouldn't change their minds, so finally Ambrose decided that it must be God's will. He began to prepare.

And what big preparations he had to make. He had to be baptized and confirmed, receive the Eucharist, be ordained a priest, and be made a bishop, all in one week!

As it turned out, Ambrose made the right decision when he accepted the people's choice as God's will. He was an excellent bishop. He gave all of his wealth to the poor. He studied hard so he could teach people the truth about Jesus. Ambrose became such a popular preacher that he gained the nickname "honey tongued." Of course, Ambrose is the patron saint of bees!

Ambrose had been an excellent leader of the city, brave and fair. As bishop, he was just as brave. He was never afraid to stand up to leaders when they broke God's laws.

When Ambrose had been bishop for about fifteen years, Emperor Theodosius became angry with the people who lived in a city called Thessalonica. They had killed the governor of their city, and Theodosius decided to punish them. While the people were watching chariot races in their city's coliseum, Theodosius ordered his soldiers to go out among the crowd and kill as many of the people as they could in revenge for the governor's death. By the end of the day, seven thousand people lay dead because of the emperor's order.

Ambrose was outraged. He wrote to the emperor immediately and told him that he was not allowed to even step inside a church again until he had done serious penance for this horrible sin. Do you know how brave Ambrose was to do that? The emperor had just had thousands of people murdered—he could just as easily have gotten rid of one outspoken bishop.

But he didn't. Theodosius realized how wrong he had been, and he did as Ambrose said. It's been said that there was never a day for the rest of his life that the emperor did not regret his terrible sin. Ambrose was at his side when he died.

Ambrose was afraid when the people elected him bishop of Milan, and he couldn't imagine that he was the right person for the job. But when the people continued to believe in him, Ambrose understood that God was speaking through their support.

So the next time you're asked to do something hard, remember the brave and kind bishop Ambrose, who said yes even though he was afraid.

St. Ambrose was surprised that the people of Milan asked him to be their bishop. Are you sometimes surprised by what other people think your gifts and talents are?

St. Gregory the Great *540–604*

September 3

"We're moving."

Of all the things parents can say, isn't this one of the worst? If you've ever had to move to a new town or state, you know how hard it is, and if you haven't, you can probably imagine.

You have to leave behind everything you know and start all over: new room, new neighborhood, new school, and new friends. It's a really hard change to make.

But maybe you've noticed something else. After a while, everything's okay.

Sure, it's different, and you miss your old friends, but the new ones are okay. In fact, the new friends might be pretty great.

What you might have noticed is that although the change was hard, good things came out of it. You've met people you never would have met. And you've done things you never would have tried if you had stayed where you were.

Change is hard, but change can be a really good thing too.

St. Gregory the Great's life involved a lot of change. Some changes he chose to make, and some of them he didn't.

Gregory chose to make the first change in his life. He had been born into a wealthy Roman family. By the time he was a young man, he had been so successful that he was the prefect of Rome. That means that Gregory did the kind of job a mayor does today.

Rome was in terrible shape in the sixth century. It had been attacked many times over the past two hundred years. The city had been built so that more than a million people could live there, but when Gregory was alive, only about forty thousand did. It was almost like a ghost town.

Invaders had cut the running water supply. The great buildings of Rome—such as the Colosseum—were unused and empty. People were very poor, not only in the city but all over Italy. They suffered terribly from hunger and sickness.

Gregory did his best, as leader, to help the people of Rome. But after a few years, he made a change in his life because he felt that God was calling him to be something new.

Gregory, the rich young leader of Rome, sold all of the land he owned and gave most of the money to the poor. With the rest, he started six monasteries and turned his own beautiful home into a monastery as well.

Then Gregory became a monk.

That's a big change, isn't it? Just wait—there are more changes to come.

Gregory wanted to lead the life of a monk. He wanted to spend his days praying, learning, and helping the poor who came to the monastery for help. But the people in Rome didn't forget Gregory and what a good leader he was.

A few years after Gregory became a monk, great rains and floods almost destroyed Rome. The floods brought diseases, and many people died, including the pope.

The Romans were desperate. The pope had been one of the few leaders in the city, and now he was dead. They needed a strong leader to help them survive the diseases and the poverty the floods had brought.

St. Gregory the Great

What about Gregory?

It made sense to the people, but Gregory wasn't happy about the idea. It was too big of a change. He had worked before as a leader in the city and in the church, and he hadn't liked it much. He much preferred the quiet life of the monastery.

But the people and priests of Rome elected Gregory as their pope anyway. He argued with them, he tried to hide, and he even wrote to the emperor asking him to reject the election. He didn't, so Gregory became the pope.

It was certainly a big change and one that Gregory hadn't chosen. But Gregory soon decided that God had spoken through the people's vote. He had been given the chance to help a lot of people, and he would use it.

Gregory had always been more concerned about the poor than about anything else. The church owned a lot of land, and Gregory used the profits from the crops grown on this land to help the hungry people of Rome.

One day, many years before he became pope, Gregory had seen some slaves being sold in a market in Rome. They looked different from the Romans. They had light hair and skin. Gregory asked where they were from, and he was told that they came from an island many miles north of Italy. Today, we call that island Great Britain.

When he became pope, Gregory remembered those slaves and wondered if their land had ever heard the good news of Jesus' love. He sent missionaries to share that message.

Gregory also helped bring peace to the people of Rome and Italy. He wrote books filled with wisdom and guidance. He was very interested in the Mass and especially in the music that was used during Mass. For hundreds of years, Catholic masses used a style of music called "Gregorian chant." It was named after Pope Gregory, who worked to make sure that the Mass was always celebrated with joy and reverence.

Gregory helped so many people while he was pope that he is one of only three popes to have "the Great" attached to his name.

St. Gregory had a hard time with some of the changes he had to make in his life. But just like you can, he used these changes as chances to grow and become stronger. He understood that God was always with him and that God could help him use even the hardest changes to do the most good!

St. Gregory's life didn't follow the road he thought it would. Can you think of some ways in which surprising changes have brought good things into your life?

St. Francis of Assisi *1181–1226*

October 4

You've got a room stuffed with toys and games and your own television.

Why change?

You have lots of good times with your friends at the movies and at the mall. Why change?

You've got a busy schedule filled with lessons, sports practice, and club meetings. Why change?

If you have all the stuff you want, you're comfortable, and you go to bed every night under warm blankets and with your head on a soft pillow, why change?

Hundreds of years ago, the people of a little Italian city named Assisi asked one of their favorite sons, Francis, those kinds of questions. It was long before televisions and malls, but his pleasures had been much the same: comfort and parties, success and a bright future.

But now he was wandering around town in a torn robe, barefoot and with a shaved head. He stood at their doors and under their windows with a great big smile on his face, singing songs about God and asking for crusts of bread. Rumor was that he took care of lepers. Rumor was that he was trying to rebuild an old church outside of town all by himself.

What had happened? Why had Francis changed?

Francis had not been born to wear ragged clothes and beg for his food. His father bought and sold beautiful fabrics, and this had brought wealth to their family. Francis was dearly loved by his Italian father and French mother. Some people said he was spoiled.

Everyone in Assisi loved Francis. He spent money like mad on good times for himself and for all of his friends. Francis was the one who organized parties. He composed and sang beautiful songs in his clear, strong voice. He dressed in the latest fashions.

And like most young men of his day, Francis was always ready for adventure. These were the days of knights in shining armor, damsels in distress, and castles filled with gold. Back before Francis started wandering around in tattered robes, he had wanted to be a knight. He had gone off to war.

Francis went into battle twice. The first time, he and his company, which was full of his friends, attacked a neighboring town. It wasn't anything like Francis expected. It wasn't glamorous and glorious. It was bloody and deadly, miserable and sad. His side lost the battle, and some of his friends were killed. Francis was taken prisoner.

His father got him out of prison and brought him home, but Francis wasn't quite the same. He'd fallen ill in prison, and for a little while Francis slowed down.

But not for long. Soon Francis was back to normal, having good times again and spending his money on fine clothes and good wine.

The chance to fight another battle came up, this time far away. Francis decided he would go, but this time with only a boy (called a squire) to help him.

Francis's father spent a lot of money on a beautiful suit of armor for his son. And so Francis went off, covered from head to toe in the finest armor money could buy.

A day out of Assisi, Francis stopped for the night. He took off his heavy armor and lay down to go to sleep, hoping to dream of the glorious battles he would soon meet and the praises people would sing about his courage.

Francis did dream that night. But it was a different kind of dream. It was more like a voice, very strong and very real. The voice asked Francis what he was going to do, and Francis answered.

The voice spoke again and asked, "Who can give you more, the master or the servant?"

"The master!" Francis answered.

"Then why are you abandoning the master for the servant?"

What do you think this meant?

Francis was giving his life to doing what other people wanted and thought was important. That voice—you know whose voice it was now, don't you?—asked him a very sensible question.

Why spend your time doing what other people want when you could be doing what God, the master of all, wants?

So Francis changed. He didn't turn around completely, all at once, but he took little steps as he grew to understand the full meaning of Jesus' teaching. The hard thing for Francis, of course, was that every little step he took to be closer to his heavenly Father pushed him away from what his earthly father believed was important, and this caused terrible conflict.

First, Francis sold his beautiful armor and his horse, and he returned home to Assisi. He didn't have much to say to his angry father, but everyone could tell that something was just a little bit different.

Francis lived at home for a while. But even while he stayed in his family's house, he started doing odd things. He prayed a lot more. He put away his fine wardrobe and wore simple clothes. He stopped going to parties. He spread out all the family's bread on the table and invited the poor people of the town to come in and eat their fill.

Francis had changed, and it was making people nervous, especially his father. But there were even more changes to come.

As Francis listened to God more and more, he gradually understood what God wanted for him. Jesus had said many times in the Gospels that the stuff you own is not important at all. Jesus said that money and things can even come between you and God.

Jesus told us that we can find true happiness only in God.

Francis decided to believe Jesus completely. That meant that Francis would give everything up. He wouldn't own anything. He'd live only for God and on God's love, as Jesus did.

As you can imagine, this change of attitude and lifestyle didn't make Francis's father happy at all. In fact, he was embarrassed, enraged, and almost crazy with fury. He really snapped the day Francis sold several bolts of material from his fabric shop to get money to rebuild an abandoned church outside of town, a church called San Damiano.

For weeks, the people of Assisi watched the family's troubles just as people today watch a soap opera on television, holding their breath and wondering what would happen next. They could hear through their open windows and doors the sound of Francis's father beating him. They could hear the silence when he locked Francis in a closet as a punishment for his rebellion.

Francis's mother let him out, but his father soon found him and raged at Francis again. He grabbed him roughly and dragged him through the narrow streets of Assisi to the town square. He wanted the leaders of Assisi to force Francis to give back the money he'd lost when Francis sold the fabrics and put the profits into that old church.

Francis knew the time had come. If he didn't do something now, at this moment, this terrible conflict would never end. His father would never understand anyway, so it was time to go ahead and take that final step.

So in front of the people of Assisi, his parents, and the bishop, Francis made the biggest change of all. He started by stepping right out of his clothes. He stood quietly and looked at his family.

"'Our Father, who art in heaven,'" Francis said. "God is my only father now. I return to you everything I have received—the money and the clothes too."

It was as if Francis were being born all over again, this time as God's child. God was the only one Francis had to obey now. And so Francis walked away, covered now by a shirt someone had dug out of the garbage.

That was fine with Francis. He didn't need anything more in order to spend the rest of his life serving God alone. He tended to the poorest of the poor, kissing and blessing lepers, whom no one else could even bear to look at. He wandered around the country, owning nothing, happy as a lark, singing and preaching about God's love.

He blessed all of creation, bringing calm to even the wildest beasts, such as the wolf he convinced to stop terrorizing a village. He invented a beautiful, brand-new way of celebrating Christmas: by recreating the stable and manger where Jesus was born. We call this the Nativity scene.

And at the end of his life, holy Brother Francis had grown so close to Jesus that the stigmata, the wounds of Jesus' crucifixion, appeared on Francis's own hands and feet.

Francis did all of this with joy. Everyone who met him felt the deepest happiness they'd ever felt. It was a happiness that was so contagious that others were moved to join him, forming a new kind of religious order called the Franciscans.

Francis could have stayed rich and spent the rest of his life getting richer. But instead he listened. He listened to the voice that told him that someday the fabric would rot, the gold would run out, and his young body would grow old and sick.

He listened to God's voice in his heart, promising him a joy that would never fade.

St. Francis of Assisi listened to God and made big changes in his life. When we listen carefully to God, we can sometimes hear the same encouragement. What changes do you think God might be calling you to make?

St. Ignatius of Loyola *1491–1556*

July 31

Sometimes change is scary.

Even if you know a big change is for the best, it can still be scary. For instance, you know that there must be a better way to spend your time than sitting in front of the television or playing computer games. You know that God created you for more than that. But it's scary to even think about changing. You're just so used to plopping yourself down in that chair and turning off your brain.

If you didn't do what you're so used to doing, what would you do with your time? What would happen if you actually used your mind and your creativity during all those hours instead of putting them to sleep?

Just think—if you really tried to start living God's way instead of the world's, anything could happen. You might not be able to do it. You might not be yourself anymore. That funny, curious, energetic person you thought you were might become boring.

It's okay to have these worries. But the stories of saints show us that we shouldn't worry about change. Just look at St. Ignatius of Loyola.

Ignatius lived in Spain during the sixteenth century. It was a time of kingdoms and battles, armies and soldiers.

From the time he was a teenager, Ignatius had been a soldier. His life was full of adventure and excitement. He spent a lot of time in the palaces of dukes and princes. He was strong and full of life. Ignatius believed in God, but he didn't do much about his faith. He didn't do much more than go to Mass and say his prayers. He spent his spare time doing things that weren't exactly admirable. He used his time and his talents for his own glory and pleasure and not much else.

Ignatius had been living this way for a long time when one spring day he found himself in a frightening position. He was fighting with an army of fellow Spaniards, and they were in a battle with the French. The French had taken all the land around the Spaniards except for one little spot. Ignatius and another soldier held on to that bit of land, which was high on a hill, inside a fort. Everyone else wanted to surrender because there was really no chance that they could win.

Ignatius stood before the troops. He called out to his friends in a clear, strong voice. They couldn't surrender! They had the protection of the fort, and they had weapons. Why should they give up?

So the troops listened to Ignatius and continued fighting against the French. It didn't work. They lost, and Ignatius was shot.

In those days, guns didn't shoot little bullets, which are bad enough. These guns shot big, round pellets that were sometimes the size of small rocks, almost like small cannonballs. That's what blasted through Ignatius's hip and went straight through his leg and down to his other knee. This was a very serious injury.

But, as always, Ignatius was brave. He was strong on the painful journey back to his home, even as he was carried over rough roads, his shattered leg bumping harshly with every step. He was strong when doctors discovered that his leg had been set incorrectly and told him that unless his leg was rebroken and reset, he would never walk again.

When Ignatius's leg finally started to heal properly, he discovered two things. One of his bones was still sticking out, forming an ugly bump under his knee. And the leg that had been broken was now shorter than the other one.

So Ignatius decided he would be strong again. He insisted that the doctors saw off that ugly bump under his knee. He chained a cannonball to his short leg and spent hours each day letting it hang free, hoping the ball would stretch the leg back out to its normal size.

Back in those days, there weren't many ways to relieve pain. So this "therapy" Ignatius put himself through was probably incredibly painful and tiring. But Ignatius was a strong man.

Because he had spent all those months in his sickbed, Ignatius got bored. He asked for something to read. He was hoping for adventure books, tales that were popular back then: knights fighting for the hands of beautiful ladies, traveling to distant lands, and battling strange creatures.

But for some reason, two completely different books were brought to Ignatius. One was a book about the life of Christ, and the other was a collection of saints' stories, sort of like this book.

Ignatius read these books. He thought about them. He was struck by the great sacrifices that the saints had made for God. He was overwhelmed by their love of Jesus.

And Ignatius thought, "Why am I using my life just for myself? These people did so much good during their time on earth. Why can't I?"

Ignatius decided that he would use the talents God had given him—his strength, his leadership ability, his bravery, and his intelligence—to serve God and God's people.

While Ignatius continued to heal, he started praying very seriously. God's peace filled his heart and assured him that he was on the right path.

When Ignatius was all healed and ready to walk and travel again, he left his home to prepare for his new life. It wasn't easy. He was thirty, which was considered old in those days, and he was getting a late start in his studies for the priesthood. In those days, the Mass was said only in Latin, and Latin was the language all educated people used to communicate with each other. Ignatius didn't know a bit of Latin. So for his first Latin lessons, big, rough Ignatius had to sit in a classroom with a bunch of ten-year-old boys who were learning Latin for the first time too!

That takes a different kind of strength, doesn't it?

Ignatius continued to travel. He gathered nine friends who felt the same way he did, and together they made a promise to God. They were the founders of the Company of Jesus, also called the Jesuits.

What started with Ignatius and his nine friends grew over just a few years into a group of priests and brothers that had more than a thousand members. They used their talents to teach and preach about Jesus all over the world.

And to think it all began because one man—St. Ignatius of Loyola—was strong and brave enough to change!

St. Ignatius let God lead him to use his gifts of strength and leadership to spread the good news of Jesus, even though it meant changing his life. What are your gifts and talents? Are there ways that you could change your life to use them to help others?

St. Camillus de Lellis *1550–1614*

July 14

Do you have a bad habit?

Changing our bad habits is hard for a lot of reasons. Sometimes we think our bad habits are fun. Sometimes we

can't imagine any other way of acting or thinking. That's why we call them habits—they're hard to change.

Maybe you argue with your mom every time she asks you to do a chore. You got into the habit a long time ago, and you're so used to being that way that arguing is almost automatic. You don't know any other way of answering her. How can you break that habit and give your mom the respect she deserves?

Sometimes bad habits are difficult to change because we're convinced that this is just the way we are. We lie so much that we become liars, and we think it's hopeless to even try to start telling the truth. We're so used to avoiding chores that we decide that it's just the way we are and nothing can change us. We decide we can't be any better. We decide there's no hope for us.

But isn't there always hope?

St. Camillus de Lellis lived for a long time with no hope. He led such a wandering, selfish life for so long that he didn't think anything could ever change him.

Camillus's mother was old when he was born. She was almost sixty years old, and she died when Camillus was only a teenager.

Camillus's father had not been around very much. His father was a soldier, a heavy drinker, and a gambler. Being around someone like that doesn't sound like the best life for a kid. But when his mother died, Camillus had no choice but to go find his father.

Although Camillus's father was a soldier, he didn't serve any one country. He was what is called a soldier of fortune. Rather than fight for a principle or a cause, he would simply fight for whoever would pay him. He'd fight for a king, a prince, or a duke, anywhere, anytime, as long as he was given a tent over his head and a few coins to spend or gamble with.

So when Camillus was seventeen, he chose this way of life too. He traveled with his father, fighting all over Europe and in the Middle East. When there were no battles to fight, they went to towns and made money gambling on card games.

Camillus kept on living this way even after his father died, which happened just a few years after Camillus went to live with him. Every once in a while Camillus would have time to think. He'd wonder if this was really the best way to spend his life. Once, when his leg got badly hurt, he went to work in a hospital, since that was the only way he could afford to have his leg treated. He tried for a while to be good, but it didn't last long. His bad habits returned, and before long he was gambling with the other patients and causing fights. The hospital threw him out.

Was there any hope for Camillus de Lellis? He was a grown man now. He was used to living one way: fighting in wars, gambling, and getting into more fights. It seemed as if these habits were too deep to ever break.

A soldier of fortune can have good luck and bad luck, depending on what side has hired him to fight. It's the same kind of risk that gamblers take, and Camillus was both. As the years went on, Camillus's luck got worse and worse. Once, in a card game, he gambled away almost every piece of clothing he had and had to beg outside a church for money.

A rich man came out of the church. He looked at Camillus, who was very tall, and wondered why such a strong young man would be begging for his living instead of working. Camillus had no answer. He just quietly accepted the man's money. The man gave Camillus a note that told him where he could find work. Camillus stuffed the note in his pocket.

He thought about going to accept this work, but his friend, who was also a gambler, convinced him that it wouldn't be any fun. They started down the road in the other direction, but suddenly Camillus stopped. He couldn't go on. This was no way to live. His bad habits were deep indeed, but Camillus realized that no habit was too deep to break, especially with God's help. Maybe God had been trying to help him through the offer of the kind man at the church.

So Camillus broke away from his friend and ran. He ran twelve miles back to the town. He pulled the paper out of his pocket and studied it. Where was this work?

The note led him to a monastery.

The monks needed workers to help them build their monastery. For the first few weeks, Camillus worked only to earn money to help him through the winter.

But after being around the monks for so long and seeing how peaceful they were, Camillus began to think. He began to pray too, and soon Camillus found the strength to change. This time, he really did change.

Camillus let God's love into his heart. He started to believe that God loved him even though he had been a terrible sinner. Camillus understood that this great gift of love was meant to be shared. He decided that he would share God's love with those who were troubled by the same problems he'd suffered from for so long.

He knew what it was like to be poor and desperate and sick, with no money for a hospital or doctor. He had lived that way for a very long time. That's where his bad habits had taken him. So Camillus dedicated the rest of his life to helping the sick.

Even though he was older than most who were on that path, he began his serious religious studies. When he was thirty-four, he was ordained a priest, and he even started his own religious order. He and his brothers looked in the poorest parts of the cities, in the darkest corners, and in the dirtiest basements to find people who were sick, hurt, and too poor to get help. They took these people to their hospitals, cleaned them up, and gave them the best treatment they could. While they did this work, they wore clothes with a special symbol sewn on them: a red cross. Today, that red cross is still the symbol for medical care everywhere in the world.

This is how much Camillus let himself be filled with God's love. Once, two ships came into the city harbor. The ships were filled with sailors suffering from the plague—a deadly disease that had no cure. The sailors weren't allowed to leave the ships, and no one wanted to go on board to help them.

Except Camillus and his brothers. They boarded the ships. They helped the miserable victims of the plague. They risked their own lives to help, and indeed, two of Camillus's brothers died.

If you'd met Camillus when he was a young man, you would have never believed what he would become, would you? You would have never believed that this ragged man who spent his days fighting and his nights gambling would, in just a few years, be cheerfully and bravely helping the sick.

You would have thought Camillus's habits were too deep to break. You would have thought there was no way he could ever change.

But with God, all things are possible, aren't they?

When St. Camillus de Lellis let God help him break his sinful habits, he found great happiness. What bad habits do you have that you'd like God to help you break?

St. Katharine Drexel *1858–1955*

March 3

We're always trying to get more, aren't we?

We wander through the mall, pointing at items in store windows, wishing we had enough money for that computer game or those CDs. Then we page through magazines, looking at the ads for clothes, makeup, and the latest cool toys and wishing we had some of that stuff too.

Don't forget television. Don't forget the commercials filled with bright colors, loud music, and lots of happy kids telling you, "You gotta have it!"

Grown-ups want more too. A pay raise. A better job. A bigger house. Maybe even that super-lucky lottery ticket.

It's all about *more*. We've got to get more stuff. Then we'll really be happy.

Really?

Think about this: A young woman wakes up one morning to find that she's got millions and millions of dollars—all hers, to spend on whatever she wants. There's no question in her mind. She's going to spend, and she's going to spend big.

But she's not going to spend the way most people would. She's going to spend the rest of her life giving that money away.

This is a true story. It's the story of our newest American saint, Katharine Drexel, a woman who was born into wealth and who couldn't wait to give it all away.

Katharine was born in Philadelphia to a family of wealth and power. Her grandfather and then her father had built a fortune in banking. Katharine lived with her mother and father and sister. When Katharine was just a month old, her mother died. Not long after, her father remarried, and he and his new wife had another daughter. That made three Drexel sisters in all.

It seems that giving was in the Drexel blood. Katharine's parents were quite generous. Katharine's stepmother, Emma, was beloved among the poor of Philadelphia for the help she offered. Twice a week she'd open the Drexels' back gate to the poor, and she'd spend her day filling any need that was brought to her, be it food, shoes, or money for rent or medicine. Emma also paid rent every single month for the apartments of 150 families.

It was a happy life, filled with comfort, travel, and lots of generous giving. Sadness came, though, as it does to all families, and it came to the Drexels all at once.

In 1883, when Katharine was twenty-five, her stepmother died, and two years later, her father died. The three Drexel girls were all alone.

After the sadness and shock had worn off, the young women had to think about their lives. They had been left a fortune— fourteen million dollars. What would they do with it?

They knew right away. They would follow their family tradition of giving. The oldest, Elizabeth, used her share to build orphanages for boys. The youngest, Louise, spent much of her money on schools for African American children.

That leaves us with the middle child, Katharine.

Katharine would certainly continue her family's tradition of giving. She wouldn't make any changes there. But another part of her life would change drastically.

Katharine would give up her life of comfort. She'd give up a future that could have been filled with fancy homes, parties, and beautiful clothes. Katharine would become a nun. Not only that, she'd start her very own religious community.

Here's what happened. After her father died, Katharine became interested in the problems of African Americans and Native Americans. In those days, African Americans were still recovering from the horrors of slavery, and they faced a great deal of prejudice and discrimination. Many Native Americans were suffering too. They had been driven from their homes by the American government and had been forced to live on reservations. Many suffered in desperate poverty and sickness, and their children had a great need for good schools and teachers who cared about them.

Katharine traveled to Rome and got to meet the pope. During their talk, Katharine told the pope about the problems of the poor people of these two minority groups. She asked him to send European nuns and priests to America to help them.

But the pope had another idea. Why didn't Katharine become that missionary herself?

Well, the idea had occurred to Katharine before, but she'd never received much encouragement from anyone. People had told her that such a life would be too great of a change for her.

Katharine prayed. She looked at the situation. She thought about her own gifts and talents and about how she felt God wanted her to use them.

The decision was clear. Katharine would indeed become a nun. She'd even take her decision one step further. Katharine would start her own religious congregation, called the Sisters of the Blessed

Sacrament. Serving African Americans and Native Americans would be their only work.

It wasn't an easy job. When Katharine and the sisters started their schools, they often received threats from hateful people. These people didn't want to see minorities educated. They didn't want them to get good jobs.

But despite the threats, Sister Katharine Drexel continued to work. She founded a school in Santa Fe, New Mexico, for Native Americans. Then she founded a school in Virginia for African American girls. In all, Sister Katharine was responsible for starting forty-nine elementary schools and twelve high schools. She also started one university—Xavier University in New Orleans, which was built especially to give African American students an excellent college education.

Sister Katharine lived for a long time. She died in 1955 at the age of ninety-seven. During her long life, she spent every bit of her share of the family fortune.

But she didn't spend it on herself. She could have bought anything she wanted—the most beautiful clothes, the most fascinating new trinkets, trips around the world, and rooms in the most luxurious hotels.

But St. Katharine Drexel looked to Jesus—and found a better way.

St. Katharine Drexel made unexpected changes in her life that helped others. How do you think it feels to make a change like that?

 # PART 12

SAINTS ARE

People Who Are Brave

*Whoever wishes to come after me
must deny himself, take up his cross,
and follow me.*

Matthew 16:24

St. Perpetua and St. Felicity *d. 203*

March 7

If someone wanted to find you next Sunday morning, where would that person go?

To church, maybe? I'm not surprised. You've probably gone there almost every Sunday since you were small. You've gotten out of bed, dressed in your nicest clothes, gone to church, and sat with your family in the pew. You've prayed, sung, and talked to your friends afterward. Then you've gotten back in the car and gone out to lunch or back home.

You probably don't even think about it too much. It's just a normal, routine part of life. You like it, even though sometimes you complain.

Well, stop and think for a moment. Can you imagine living in a time and in a land in which doing that very ordinary thing—going to worship Jesus—was against the law?

Can you imagine having to keep your faith in Jesus an absolute secret? Wouldn't it be a strange, scary thing to wake up every day knowing that if your Christian faith was discovered, you could be arrested and even killed by the government?

Believe it or not, many Christians throughout history lived this way, and some still do even today. In fact, for much of the first three hundred years after Jesus came, this was exactly the way Christians had to live. They knew that if they were true to their faith in Christ, the leaders of the Roman Empire could arrest, torture, and kill them.

Following Christ is never easy, but it takes special bravery when you could die for believing. It takes special courage to tell the truth when you know that a simple lie—just a few words—could spare your life. Perpetua and Felicity had just that kind of courage.

Perpetua was twenty-two years old. She was married and had a baby son. Felicity was a slave girl who was very close to giving birth to her own baby. She was eight months pregnant.

Perpetua and Felicity were among a group of catechumens who lived in Carthage, a city in northern Africa. Catechumens are people who have committed themselves to faith in Jesus but haven't been baptized yet. Perpetua knew that their group was being watched by the Roman government. The government leaders were waiting for a reason to arrest them for being Christians. Perpetua's father knew it too. He tried to discourage her from being honest about what she believed.

She asked him to look at a water pitcher sitting on the table. Could he call it anything but what it was? Could he call it a dog or a plate?

No, he couldn't. In the same way, Perpetua reminded her father, she could never call herself anything but what she was: a Christian.

Soon after Perpetua, Felicity, and the other catechumens were baptized, they were arrested. In their dark stone prison, the group, accused of the crime of believing in Christ, awaited their trial. Felicity prayed for her child to be born safely and soon. Perpetua prayed for her son to be brought to her so that she could care for him herself until their sentence was passed. He was eventually brought to her. With her little son in her arms, the prison was "made a palace for me." We know she said this because she wrote it in a letter that we can still read today.

The day of the trial arrived. Perpetua's father begged her one more time to just offer a sacrifice to the Roman gods so that her life would be spared. But Perpetua answered simply, "I am a

Christian." She had to tell the truth about who she was and what she believed. How can you lie about who you are and still have peace in your heart?

The whole group of new Christians was condemned and sentenced. Their punishment? Just because they were Christians, they would be fed to wild beasts in a public arena for the entertainment of all the people of Carthage.

The days passed in prison. Felicity gave birth to her daughter, whom she sent to be raised by her sister. Perpetua knew she would never see her son again. But as the group prayed, their faith grew stronger. They knew that Jesus was waiting for them on the other side of death.

Isn't it strange that people were arrested and killed simply for what they believed? Even stranger was that their deaths were entertainment for the thousands of people who gathered in the arena that warm March afternoon.

The men were killed first. Leopards, bears, and a wild boar were brought out to tear them to pieces. The crowds cheered and wanted more. They fell silent when they saw two young women, Perpetua and Felicity, stripped of all their clothes and brought out for the final act. Felicity had given birth just three days before. We might wonder if the crowd felt ashamed, just for a moment, of what they were asking for.

If so, their shame didn't last. Perpetua and Felicity were put in robes and then covered with nets. A wild, crazed cow was brought out from the darkness of the arena. She immediately attacked them both but didn't kill them.

Finally, a sword was used to end the brave women's lives. Those who recount the story tell us that more than a few witnesses, including the jailer himself, started believing in Jesus because of these two strong young women.

It would have been easy for Perpetua and Felicity to say, "No, I don't believe." It would have been easy for them and every one of the thousands of Christians threatened by the Romans to just offer a sacrifice and walk away. By pretending that they weren't friends with Jesus after all, their lives would have been safe and sound. They could have lived as if Jesus wasn't worth telling the truth about.

Yes, they could have done that. What do you think would have happened to *our* faith if they had?

St. Perpetua and St. Felicity could have saved their lives by lying about their faith. What kinds of things do we sometimes try to "save" by lying about our faith?

St. George *d. 303*

April 23

What's standing between you and Jesus?

What's keeping you from being close to him? Are you scared of what other kids will say? Are you afraid that you'll have to give up some bad habits?

Or is it that you really want to be closer to Jesus but just don't know how?

All of these problems may seem like frightening dragons that breathe fire and stand between you and a precious treasure. You're going to have to be brave to defeat those dragons, aren't you?

Following Jesus takes courage. For hundreds of years, Christians have known this. That's why, for hundreds of years, Christians have honored the brave St. George.

We don't know much about the real St. George. We know that he was from the country that's now called Turkey. Back in those days, that land was part of the Roman Empire, and George was a Roman soldier.

George was also a Christian—and a proud one. He didn't make any secret of his loyalty to Jesus. That angered his superiors, and eventually George was killed for being a Christian. We don't have any record of exactly how he died. But soon after his death, people in his hometown started honoring George for his courageous faith. That tells us that he must have suffered terribly yet stayed faithful to Jesus through it all.

Stories of George's courage spread. All through Europe, churches were named after him and his feast day was celebrated. George became especially popular in England. He's even the patron saint of England. He's also the patron saint of the Boy Scouts.

For hundreds of years, people wrote poems and sang songs about the brave St. George. They used their imaginations to explain how brave he was and what kind of courage it takes to follow Jesus. One of the most famous stories is of St. George and the dragon.

According to this story, there was a village that was terrorized by a huge, fierce dragon. He breathed fire. His breath also had horrible germs in it that made people sick. The people of the village were helpless before the power of the dragon.

The only way they could keep the dragon from destroying them completely was to give him two sheep a day. Of course, it wasn't long before they ran out of sheep, so they had to find another way to keep the dragon happy. Something else—a person—would have to be sacrificed to the dragon.

The people of the village decided that the only fair way to pick a person was to choose by lots. That means that they did something like drawing straws, and whoever drew the shortest straw would go to the dragon. One day, the shortest straw was drawn by the king's daughter.

The princess was traveling to the outside of the village, weeping, when George happened to pass by. He asked her why she was so sad, and she told him. George decided that there was no way this princess, or any other person, would die because of the dragon.

Many people had tried to defeat the dragon before, but none had succeeded. George was told to be sneaky and sly with the dragon and to try to trick him, but he refused. He would face the dragon directly, without fear.

And he did. George made the sign of the cross and asked God for strength. The dragon emerged from his cave, breathing fire, growling, and charging. George didn't think twice. He took his lance and plunged it deep into the dragon's body.

The dragon wasn't dead yet, though, and George wasn't finished. He put the princess's belt around the dragon's neck and led it, limping and weak, into the village. The people ran and screamed in fear, but George told them to not be afraid—it was with God's help that he had done this. If the people would accept God's help, be baptized, and help the poor of their village, George would slay the dragon and free them from its cruel power forever.

The people of the village gladly put their faith in God, and George killed the dragon once and for all. That's why almost every picture you see of St. George shows him standing victorious over a dragon.

And that's why we're reminded of St. George when we think of what brave Christians can do.

Our dragons don't breathe fire. They make fun of us for going to church. They whisper that we're so bad that God could never love us. They tell us that religion is just for grown-ups. They scare us into thinking that following Jesus is just too hard.

So when those kinds of dragons scare you, just imagine you're St. George, filled with God's power and love, and nothing—not even a frightening dragon—can ever keep you from Jesus!

St. George bravely faced a dragon that was causing great harm. Can you think of some dragons that are trying to scare you away from following Jesus?

St. Margaret Clitherow *1556–1586*

March 26

Perhaps you've been blessed with good neighbors.

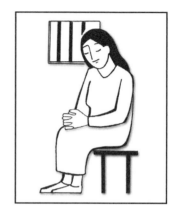

You know how helpful they can be, don't you? Good neighbors watch your house when you're gone. They lend you a hedge clipper or a few cups of flour when you need it. They probably even keep an eye on you to help your parents make sure you're safe all the time.

But that's not the end of it. You may know about some of the good things your neighbors do, but often there's more than meets the eye—your neighbor probably does all kinds of nice things that you don't even know about, things that would surprise you if you did.

Let's take Mrs. Clitherow, for example. If you had lived next door to Mrs. Clitherow, you would have thought she was a nice neighbor.

She worked hard, like everyone else in the neighborhood. She helped with her husband's butcher shop even though she wasn't crazy about the bloody work. She was also a loving mother to her children.

Yes, you would have liked Mrs. Clitherow. But you probably would have been surprised to discover that there was more to Margaret Clitherow than just a busy life of work and care for others. You wouldn't have believed what was going on in her house.

Behind those thick walls and heavy doors—day after day and week after week for years—Mrs. Clitherow was breaking the law.

Mrs. Clitherow was a Catholic.

You see, if Margaret Clitherow were your neighbor, you'd be living in York, England, in the late 1500s. At that time, England was going through some big changes. Until recently, England had been a Catholic country for hundreds of years. But a few years before our story begins, King Henry VIII had rejected the authority of the pope and had broken away from the Catholic Church. Now Henry's daughter, Queen Elizabeth, was the head of this new church, called the Church of England, and under her rule, being a Catholic was a crime.

That's right. Back then it was illegal to teach children about the Catholic faith. It was illegal to go to Mass. It was illegal to let a Catholic priest come inside your house.

Margaret Clitherow broke all those laws. She even went to jail for breaking them. She didn't care, because she knew they were wrong.

Margaret hired a Catholic tutor to teach her children about the Catholic faith. He came to their home, in secret, to teach Margaret's children and other Catholic children.

Margaret hosted the Mass in her home for her family and her Catholic neighbors. Whenever she got word that a priest would be coming to town, Margaret would let him stay in a secret part of her house. When the word spread, her Catholic friends would gather at Margaret's house. They would take out the vestments, prayer books, and candles that Margaret kept in a locked closet. And they would attend the Mass, which the priest offered right there, in the dark of night.

Margaret's family and friends kept her secret for a long time, but the day came when it was revealed. The police threatened a little boy who was being taught in Margaret's home. The boy was so frightened that he told the police everything.

Margaret was arrested and put in jail for her faith.

The judge wanted to have a trial, but Margaret had a surprise for him. She refused to enter a plea. That means that she wouldn't claim to be either guilty or not guilty. She did this for two reasons. First, it let the judge know that she didn't think she had done anything wrong.

But the second reason was more important. If Margaret entered a plea, there would be a trial, and her husband and children would be called in to court to testify against her. Margaret loved her family very much, and she couldn't imagine putting her husband, her two sons, or her daughter in that terrible position.

So, without a trial, Margaret was convicted of being a Catholic and was sentenced to death.

March 25, 1586, was the day of Margaret's execution. She had spent her time in prison praying and remembering how much God loved her and how God would love her forever. Because of this, Margaret wasn't afraid, even though the death that awaited her would be horrible, painful, and slow.

Margaret was laid in a shallow pit in the ground. As she lay in the pit, praying, a heavy door was laid on top of her. Slowly, enormous rocks were placed on top of the door, one by one. As the door grew heavier, Margaret's body was crushed. But before she died, Margaret whispered her final words: "Jesu, Jesu, Jesu, have mercy on me."

If you had lived next door to Margaret Clitherow, you would have known that she was a good neighbor and a good friend. But wouldn't you have been surprised to learn that she was also so brave that she wouldn't let even death scare her off from what she knew was true?

Isn't it amazing what extraordinary things ordinary people can do?

St. Margaret Clitherow

St. Margaret Clitherow was a good neighbor whose goodness extended beyond the ordinary. Can you think of other ordinary people who have done deeds of extraordinary goodness and bravery?

St. Isaac Jogues *1607–1646*

October 19

Would you ever consider
helping a person who
would probably hurt you?

Would it ever even cross
your mind?

Say there are some kids in
your neighborhood who have been mean to you for a long time.
They've decided that you and your friends don't deserve respect.
When you pass them on the street or in school, they always make
fun of you.

But suppose you've heard something about these kids. You've
heard that some of them aren't doing well in school. In fact, they're
coming close to flunking math, a subject you're really good at.

Would you go to those kids and offer to help them?

You could, you know. It's not impossible. When we ask, God can
give us the strength to do anything, no matter how hard it is.

It takes a special, deep kind of courage to go where you're not
wanted. It takes a lot of love to help people who've hurt you once
and will probably hurt you again.

It's the kind of courage St. Isaac Jogues had. It's the kind of
love—God's love—that absolutely nothing can defeat.

Isaac Jogues was born in France. When he was studying for the
priesthood, he heard all about the vast New World across the sea.

Many French people—fur trappers, soldiers, adventurers, and priests—were going to this New World, especially the most northern part of it—the dark forests, cold rivers and lakes, and icy chill of Canada.

People already lived in Canada. They were Native Americans of many different tribes. Some tribes got along well with the French settlers, and others did not. Isaac heard about these native peoples, and he knew at once how much better their lives would be if they knew about Jesus. He decided he would join the company of brave priests who were leaving France to help the natives of Canada.

After he arrived, Isaac spent a few years in Montreal, which was just a little settlement then. But soon, Isaac had the chance to travel far into the interior of Canada, to places where few Europeans had been. He would travel with a few other Frenchmen and some native guides. They would ride in canoes and walk to the place where the Huron tribes lived. There, Isaac would tell the Hurons about Jesus.

It was a hard trip, and it led to a hard life. Many of the Indians were suspicious of the Europeans. They thought they were evil spirits. They thought they brought diseases with them on purpose to kill the native people and their crops.

But Isaac worked patiently. He taught adults and children. He baptized those who needed it. He tried to help the sick as best he could. Isaac didn't want to cause hurt—he wanted to help.

To some of the Indians, Isaac's good intentions didn't matter. The members of the Mohawk tribe were the biggest enemies of the French and of members of many other native tribes. They were known as fierce warriors who treated prisoners harshly, and they were feared.

Fr. Isaac Jogues found this out for himself. He had traveled to Montreal for supplies and was coming back down the river, back to the Huron people. A group from the Mohawk tribe captured him and his companions. What followed was more than a year of terror and pain.

Once they were taken to the Mohawk settlement, Isaac was stripped of his clothes and forced to walk through a double line of villagers, who beat him with sticks and rods. They tore off his fingernails and sawed off his left thumb. They also burned him with hot coals.

Of course, the other Frenchmen and the Hurons who'd been with him were suffering the same way. They were all being tortured by the Mohawks.

The Mohawks kept Isaac as their slave for thirteen months. He had some chances to escape, but he refused because the other prisoners needed him.

But finally Isaac decided it was time to leave, and late one night he escaped from the Mohawks. He found a Dutch trading ship, which took him to the settlement of New York. From there, he found a spot on a ship sailing to England. The sailors on the ship didn't treat him very well, and by the time Isaac reached France, he was so weak and ill that many thought he would die.

But he didn't. He spent six months recovering in France, and then he made a decision. He decided to go back. He would go back to the very people who had tortured him for months and who had killed many of his friends.

It was painfully clear to Isaac that many of the natives, especially the Mohawks, needed the peaceful message of Jesus. Isaac could think of nothing more important to do with the rest of his life.

So he returned to Canada. Not many months after his return, Isaac went out with some other Frenchmen to try to make a peace treaty with some tribes. On the way back, he was captured by members of the Mohawk clan, who did not want peace.

There was no long torture this time. The end came quickly. Isaac was kept in one of the tribe's lodges, and one night he was invited to a feast. As he entered the hut, he was struck in the head with a hatchet. The attacker put Isaac's head on a stake in the village and threw his body into the river.

What Fr. Isaac Jogues did was courageous. But he had a special kind of courage. He wasn't brave because he wanted to show off or have great adventures. He was brave because he knew that those people deserved to hear the good news of Jesus. It was God's love that gave Fr. Isaac the courage to help people who had hurt him before.

It takes courage to follow Jesus. It takes courage to do the right thing. But when you think about how your words and deeds can help other people, God's love will take over and make you strong enough to follow him.

St. Isaac Jogues returned to help the people who had hurt him. Can you think of another saint in this book who did the same thing? Why would that be a hard thing to do?

The Carmelite Nuns of Compiègne

d. 1794

July 17

What does it take to be brave?

Is it physical strength? intelligence? Does being brave depend on how old you are or where you live?

There have probably been a lot of times when you've been brave. Maybe you've been brave enough to admit when you did something wrong. Perhaps you've been brave enough to stand up to a bully or someone who's spreading gossip.

You may even think back on those times and wonder where in the world you got the courage to do those brave things. When you do, you realize that your courage wasn't dependent on your size, your age, or even your brains.

You were brave because you had faith that what you were doing was right. You may not have expected that you would ever do such a brave thing—after all, your life was pretty ordinary up to that point, and even after. But somehow, the challenge to be courageous popped up out of the blue, and you met it—because you had that faith.

Our stories of saints are obviously filled with brave people who were able to stand up for the truth because they had that special faith that God wouldn't abandon his friends, no matter what.

The Carmelite Nuns of Compiègne

On a warm July day in 1794, sixteen women walked together through the streets of Paris with just that kind of faith. They came from all kinds of families. Some had rich parents, others poor. Some of the women had been to school, some had not. They were poets, musicians, and scholars. They were seamstresses, cooks, and gardeners.

But these women had one thing in common. In a few minutes, they would all die. They would be killed because they were faithful to God.

Who were these women? And who in the world would want to see them die?

The rulers of France, that's who.

In 1794, France was boiling over with violence and hate. For many years, the poor people of France had begged for fairness. The king and the other wealthy people had ignored them. In 1789, the poor and many others had revolted against the king and had started a new government they hoped would be fairer. We call this revolt the French Revolution.

But the Revolution quickly turned into a frightening, bloody time. The new rulers decided that the only way to keep their power was to kill everyone who was or might be against them. The church was one of their first victims.

Faithful Catholics were persecuted. The government took over church buildings and banned all Christian services and festivals.

Throughout all of this, a little group of nuns tried to keep praying.

They were Carmelite nuns. They lived very simply in an area called Compiègne. They spent their days working, studying, and praying a lot. They prayed that peace would return to their country.

These sixteen nuns lived this way until one day in 1792, when the police came to their convent and ordered them to leave. The government had made it a crime to be a priest, monk, or nun.

So the sixteen nuns left their convent and went to live in the city. They wore ordinary clothes and worked at ordinary jobs, but they kept praying. They prayed together in secret as often as they could.

They were able to do this for two years, until 1794, when they were found out and arrested. The trial was short and unfair. The sixteen women were condemned to die.

In those days, people were executed in public in front of huge cheering crowds. The crowds gathered in the public square around the place of execution. The guillotine loomed high above them. Once released, its razor-sharp blade would fall quickly onto the neck of the victim, cutting off her head.

The story of the nuns' execution comes to us from many witnesses. As the sixteen women walked to the place of execution, surrounded by mockery and rage, they didn't cry. They didn't shout back or try to run.

They sang. In high, pure voices they sang the Salve Regina:

Hail, Holy Queen,
Mother of Mercy,
Our light, our sweetness, and our hope.

They continued to sing as each of their sisters knelt under the blade. Gradually the crowd fell silent, watched, and listened.

Sister Charlotte was old and sick, yet she was able to forgive her executioner. The youngest sister walked up to the guillotine singing praises to God and refused to let any hand touch her as she knelt in place. All the sisters went, one by one. Their mother superior was last.

As the last person was executed, the crowd stayed silent. Usually wild cheers and drums sounded through the square, but not this time. These deaths were different. These sisters were brave and honest. The French government was wrong to make religion a crime. It was wrong to put human laws above God's law. The sisters knew this, and they would not back down from the truth. They would not pretend to agree with something that was terribly wrong just to save their lives.

As it happened, just a few days after the brave nuns of Compiègne died, this period in France's history, called the Terror, came to an end. The church was still persecuted, but a few lives were spared from the deadly guillotine, at least for a short while.

Don't you wonder how the nuns of Compiègne could be so brave?

It was their faith, wasn't it? Faith that God is real. Faith in the truth. Faith that, on the other side of the guillotine, heaven awaited, the place where these brave women could sing their beautiful hymns in peace and joy forever.

The nuns of Compiègne relied on God's promises to help them be brave. At what times in your life have you had to depend on God to help you be brave?

St. Maximilian Kolbe *1894–1941*

August 14

It takes courage to do a lot of things.

You have to be brave when you're going on a long trip by yourself for the first time. You have to be brave when you're in the hospital for an operation. You have to be brave when you're standing up to a bully.

But did you know that it takes courage to love? If you're going to love people—really love them, not just like them or enjoy them—you have to be brave.

Because, as you probably know, not everyone is going to love you back all the time. In fact, sometimes the people you are trying to love will act in pretty rotten ways.

Jesus knew that, didn't he? That's why he's always telling us to depend on him for strength. If we're going to follow Jesus and love all people as if they're our brothers and sisters (which they are!), we have to be brave. We have to be as strong and brave as Jesus was, because there will be times when we will have to love our way through pain, hurt, and very hard times.

The saints knew this, and that's why we think of them as brave people who were able to keep loving God and all of God's children no matter what, without being asked.

St. Maximilian Kolbe is a good example of a brave saint. He can teach us a great deal about that kind of love.

St. Maximilian Kolbe

Maximilian Kolbe didn't live that long ago. He was a Franciscan priest who lived in Poland in the years before World War II.

Fr. Maximilian had a lot of interests. He was very smart, and as a child he was quite interested in many topics, including outer space. Decades before rockets were launched into space, Maximilian would sit at his desk, daydreaming about space and designing ships he hoped might go there someday.

When he grew up and became a Franciscan priest, Maximilian kept dreaming about things that other people thought were impossible. Without any money, he started a Catholic magazine and newspaper that within a few years reached hundreds of thousands of people. It was so successful that Maximilian traveled across the continents to start a magazine in Japan. He didn't even speak Japanese!

Maximilian wanted to spread the good news of God's love all around the world using the fastest means and the newest inventions. Hundreds of other Franciscans joined him in Poland to do this important work.

But in 1939, the Nazis invaded Poland. After that, life would never be the same again.

The Nazis persecuted and destroyed all people who opposed their message of hate. Of course, their main target was the Jewish people, whom they wanted to wipe off the face of the earth.

Others were victims of the Nazis too, including religious people who refused to put Nazi beliefs above their belief in God. The Nazis arrested, imprisoned, and killed many priests, ministers, monks, and nuns who spoke out against their evil policies.

Because Fr. Maximilian was one of those outspoken priests, the Nazis wanted to shut down his popular magazines. In 1939, he was briefly imprisoned, then released. In 1941, the Nazis arrested him again. This time he was sent to the concentration camp at Auschwitz in Poland.

Maximilian lived in Auschwitz with thousands of other prisoners, most of them Jews. Many of them were executed in gas chambers. Maximilian, who had been sick with lung problems his whole life, lived in a large, cold building, slept on a board, and wore a blue-and-white striped prison uniform. He was forced to do hard and sometimes horrifying work, such as carrying boulders and moving large trees or carrying dead bodies to the ovens where they would be burned. He was beaten and starved. Once, a guard strapped a large, heavy plank to Fr. Maximilian's back and made him run. When he collapsed, the guard kicked him fiercely and whipped him fifty times.

But Fr. Maximilian never stopped loving God.

The prisoners who knew Fr. Maximilian and who lived through the war have written that he was always brave. He kept praying and trying to help the other prisoners. He was sad and desperate in ways you and I could never imagine. Yet he never complained.

One day, the Nazi prison guards burst into the cellblock where Maximilian lived. A prisoner had escaped, and because of this, other prisoners would be punished. The Nazis would punish them to discourage other escapes.

The furious Nazi guards selected ten prisoners. These men would be starved to death.

A cry broke the prisoners' terrified silence. "My poor wife and children! I will never see them again!"

This man who spoke, who could not hold back his grief, was Sergeant Francis Gajowniczek. Before the guards could punish him for his outburst, another voice spoke. This voice was calm and controlled.

"I would like to take the place of Sergeant Gajowniczek."

St. Maximilian Kolbe

It was Fr. Maximilian Kolbe who spoke these words. Although he hadn't been chosen to starve to death, he made the choice to starve in the sergeant's place.

He made a choice to love.

So Fr. Maximilian and the nine others were taken to the cell where they would be starved to death. In a cold, dark room with no furniture, they were stripped and left to die. For days they suffered, wept, screamed in pain, and tried to pray with Fr. Maximilian.

One by one, the men died, and every few days another corpse was taken out. After two weeks with no food and no water, four men were still alive. Fr. Maximilian was one of them.

The Nazis could wait no longer. It was time for the last four to die, so they were injected with carbolic acid, which killed them quickly. Fr. Maximilian's body was taken to the ovens and burned.

In 1982, Fr. Maximilian Kolbe was canonized a saint. Gathered with thousands of others in St. Peter's Square to listen to and watch the ceremony was one especially grateful person. Sergeant Gajowniczek, now an elderly man, stood in the crowd with his wife and children.

God's love had saved his life. God's love had worked through a single human being: St. Maximilian Kolbe, who made the brave choice to put God first.

St. Maximilian Kolbe put love for Jesus and others before his own life. Can you think of any hard steps you've taken to love in difficult situations?

PART 13

SAINTS ARE

People Who Help the Poor and Sick

*A large number of people from the
towns in the vicinity of Jerusalem
also gathered, bringing the sick . . .
and they were all cured.*

Acts of the Apostles 5:16

St. Elizabeth of Hungary *1207–1231*

November 17

Think about how much stuff you have.

Think about the toys and games in your room and the clothes in your closet. Think about how many rooms are in your house and how many cars your family drives.

Now think about what you want for Christmas or your birthday.

How much stuff do you have?

How much stuff do you want?

Elizabeth of Hungary had nearly everything she could want. True, she lived almost a thousand years ago, so she didn't have the televisions, computers, and CD players that are so important to us. But for someone living in the thirteenth century, Elizabeth had it all.

Elizabeth was a princess, and at a very young age she was promised in marriage to a prince of a neighboring country. That seems very odd to us. But among wealthy families of that time, most marriages were arranged by parents.

When she was just four years old, Elizabeth's parents sent her to live with the family of her future husband. The castle was high on a rocky mountain, and from its towers Elizabeth could look out over all the countryside and think about the future, when she herself would be queen of that land.

That day came sooner than she expected. When Elizabeth was nine years old, the prince she was promised to died, so she was promised again in marriage, this time to Ludwig, the second son. The next year, the king himself died, so Ludwig became the king. A few years later, when he was twenty-one and Elizabeth was fourteen, they were married.

Fourteen seems awfully young to be married, but in those days, men and women started their lives as grown-ups much earlier than we do now.

It was an exciting time for Elizabeth. Although she was still a girl in many ways, she was a queen, happily married to a man she loved and who loved her. When she had her children—two boys and a girl— Elizabeth's joy grew even more.

So Elizabeth had everything, didn't she? She lived in wealth and splendor. She had servants, beautiful clothes, and banquets every night.

Elizabeth could have lived just like that—rich and satisfied—for the rest of her life. She could have stayed busy in court, discussing the gossip of the day and planning the decorations for parties.

But Elizabeth couldn't do that. Even as a little girl, she'd known that the most important things were not wealth and a fancy palace. Elizabeth knew this because she had followed Jesus' teachings ever since she was a young girl.

Elizabeth knew that while Jesus spoke about many things, he talked about the poor more than almost anything else. Elizabeth knew that Jesus told many stories about how the poor were to be treated. She remembered everything Jesus had said about living on just what we need and sharing the rest with those who have nothing.

So, as best she could, Queen Elizabeth tried to follow Jesus.

Elizabeth tried, as often as she could, to dress humbly and simply. She refused to wear her crown when she went to Mass, because there was only one ruler, and that was God.

St. Elizabeth of Hungary

When Elizabeth had to host parties and banquets or preside with her husband at court, she wore her royal robes, but underneath them she always wore a rough shirt made of animal hair next to her skin. She wore this shirt to remind herself that although she was in a wealthy, powerful family, she was still a sinner just like everyone else.

But that's not all. There was no way Elizabeth could just sit still and use her wealth for herself. It would not be right, especially when so many people in the countryside needed her help. Why should she have all this extra wealth when people around her didn't even have enough to feed their children?

So Elizabeth went to work. She gave money and food to the poor, but she didn't stop there. She didn't just give and then leave. Elizabeth stepped out of that castle high on the mountain and right into the lives of people in need.

She visited the sick and bound their wounds herself. Once, she even carried a child with leprosy back to her own room in the castle. Her husband was upset at first. But when he looked at the child, he was sure that he saw Christ himself, and he understood what Elizabeth was doing.

The sick of the kingdom started coming to the castle for help, but it was a hard journey up to the top of the mountain. Elizabeth didn't want the sick to suffer any more than they already had to, so she ordered that a hospital be built at the base of the mountain. Once it was built, Elizabeth went to the hospital every day to help.

She had another hospital built too, as well as an orphanage. There wasn't any question that Elizabeth's heart was filled with the love of Jesus.

Remember this too: Elizabeth may have been a queen, but during all of this time, she was still only a teenager.

Elizabeth had children of her own, and many people in the royal family believed that helping the poor this way was not proper behavior for a queen. She had to be strong to defend her actions to her husband's family. It always takes strength to follow Jesus, and Elizabeth was a strong young woman.

Her happy marriage came to a sad end when she was only twenty. On his way to fight in a war, Ludwig fell ill with the plague and died far from home. Elizabeth was devastated.

Her life got harder in other ways too. Once Ludwig died, she was forced to leave the castle and take her children elsewhere to live. None of that stopped Elizabeth from helping, though. She continued to work for the poor, and she built one more hospital. This hospital was for people with the most terrible diseases, such as leprosy and the plague.

When she was only twenty-four, Elizabeth of Hungary died.

She was young, it's true, but she died close to Jesus and with a peaceful, happy heart. She'd done more to help the poor in a few years than most people do in a lifetime.

So think about Elizabeth of Hungary. She had everything. She lived in great comfort and luxury. She could have closed the door to that castle high on the mountain and spent her days just enjoying what she had. She could have spent her days looking at pretty pictures and listening to pretty music.

But she didn't. She looked out the window and saw hungry people. She walked down the mountain and saw the sick and the dying. She heard orphans crying, and she looked into cold, barren huts to see who needed help.

Elizabeth saw all of this and listened to Jesus. She opened her heart and spent her days and nights giving.

It's what any of us would do if we could. Isn't it?

St. Elizabeth of Hungary had great wealth and status, which she used to help others. Think of the gifts and opportunities you have. Do you use them for your own benefit or for the benefit of others?

St. Vincent de Paul *1580–1660*

September 27

There's a lot of hurt in this world, isn't there?

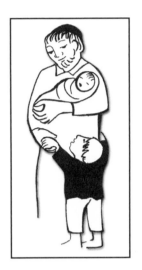

Lots of sick people, millions of hungry children, and wars that seem to never end. So many people are lonely. Others are angry and sad. All over the world people feel helpless and hopeless.

What can one person do?

A lot, that's what.

In fact, if you think about the saints in this book, you see right away that one person can do a great deal. Sometimes one person can do so much that it almost takes your breath away.

St. Vincent de Paul was one of those people who never seemed to sit still. He was so full of God's love that he couldn't stop sharing it. He was so moved by other people's hurts that he had to help every time.

All of that is amazing enough. What's more amazing is that Vincent de Paul almost didn't get a chance to do all that good work. The future almost ended for young Vincent de Paul not long after he was ordained a priest.

You'll never believe what happened.

He was kidnapped by pirates!

Sometimes we tell jokes and make funny movies about pirates. The truth is that pirates were quite real, and they were dangerous criminals. They murdered and robbed, burned ships, and took prisoners.

If your ship ever met up with pirates, you knew it was the end of you.

On the day that Fr. Vincent encountered pirates, he wasn't on a terribly important trip. He had just claimed a bit of money that his family had inherited and was going back home to France. His ship was just off the coast of France, in the Mediterranean Sea, when those most dreaded sails appeared in the distance.

The little ship Fr. Vincent was on tried to make its way to safety, but it was no use. The pirates captured it and took as prisoner everyone on board, including Fr. Vincent. Then it was off to the other shore of the Mediterranean, to hot northern Africa.

After the ship landed, Fr. Vincent and the other prisoners were given blue-and-white slave robes to wear. They were then chained together and marched up and down the streets of the town so that anyone who wanted to buy a slave could see them. People checked the prisoners' bodies as if they were animals. The prisoners were forced to run up and down the street and do other exercises to show how healthy they were.

A fisherman bought Fr. Vincent but soon resold him to an old man who practiced medicine. After a year, that man died, and Fr. Vincent was sold to a new owner. This man was a fellow Frenchman who had also been taken prisoner by African pirates, but long ago. In order to avoid slavery, this man had abandoned Christianity and had adopted the Muslim religion.

This man put Fr. Vincent to work in the hills and valleys of his farm. All day, Fr. Vincent worked in the blazing sun. He wondered if he would ever return to France, but he never complained out loud.

His owner had three wives, and one of them sometimes came to talk to Fr. Vincent. She asked him to sing for her, so he did. He sang a psalm about how much the people of Israel missed their homeland after they lost it in battle. He also sang songs about Mary.

This woman was impressed and curious. She went to her husband and wanted to know one thing. "This slave's religion is very beautiful. It was once your religion too. How could you have ever left it?"

The farmer was startled, and the question made him think hard about his life. He decided his wife was right. He had been wrong to turn his back on Jesus. He would go back to Europe and take Fr. Vincent with him.

Of course, they couldn't just say good-bye to the townspeople, hop on a boat, and start sailing. If anyone found out what was planned, both men would be killed. So they had to go in secret, in the middle of the night, escaping to the land where they could follow Jesus freely and openly.

Fr. Vincent was welcomed back in France, and it didn't take long for him to get back to work. It was almost as if nothing had ever happened to interrupt his hopes and dreams.

All around him were problems. Thousands of poor people suffered, ignored by the rich. Thousands of babies were abandoned every year by mothers and fathers who didn't think they could take care of them. Many Catholics were living selfishly, having forgotten how important Jesus said it was to help the poor and the sick. Poor people who didn't have enough money for doctors or medicine died in filth and wretchedness.

Even Fr. Vincent's fellow priests had problems. Many of them were poorly educated and were doing a terrible job of teaching and helping the people.

Fr. Vincent worked hard to fix all of these problems. He raised money to help the poor, and he set up clean, warm shelters where people who had no homes could live and learn to work. He organized the wealthy so that they could use their riches to help those in need. He started homes for abandoned babies. He worked with a group of women, most importantly St. Louise de Marillac, to serve the poor.

And Fr. Vincent never forgot what he had been. He never forgot slaves and prisoners. He raised money to buy more than a thousand slaves and bring them back to freedom in Europe.

Fr. Vincent also cared for a group of people that hardly anyone ever thought about.

Have you ever seen old movies that show hundreds of men rowing big wooden boats? The men sit on benches deep inside the boat, pushing and pulling huge oars through the water.

Well, that didn't happen only in the movies. People really used prisoners that way, and it was a miserable life. The prisoners were chained to their spots. They were fed black bread and little water. They never saw the sun, and they never bathed. They were forgotten and abandoned down there in the smelly, damp darkness.

But Vincent didn't forget them. He gave those galley slaves, as they were called, special care. He visited them, brought them extra food, and comforted them in their misery.

There is even one story that Vincent didn't want people to know. He was in a boat visiting prisoners when one man started weeping. This man had a wife. He had children. He didn't know if he would ever be able to see them again.

So Vincent de Paul took his place. It was just for a little while, just long enough for the man to escape and return home, but for that short time, Vincent de Paul took the oars himself.

St. Vincent de Paul

Not many people have done more to help the poor and sick than St. Vincent de Paul. He's remembered all around the world for his care of and mercy toward people who were suffering.

St. Vincent de Paul just couldn't walk by those people without doing something. He saw Jesus in their eyes, and he could not turn away.

Could you turn away?

St. Vincent de Paul saw the world around him as Jesus did: with compassion for the poor and sick. When you look at the world, what do you see?

St. Martin de Porres *1579–1639*

November 3

Sometimes it's really easy to feel sorry for yourself.

You get mad at life. You think that if your parents weren't so strict or if you had more money, you would be happier. You think that life would be a whole lot better if you were somehow different.

That's not a great way to think, you know.

You are who you are. Sure, you can change bad habits, and you should. With practice and care, you can also turn tiny talents into beautiful, flourishing gifts.

But wishing you were somebody else isn't the way to a peaceful heart. God made you and put you in your family at this time and in this place for a reason. You really have to trust that he knew what he was doing. You have to trust that great things are just waiting to come out of this life that's yours and yours alone.

St. Martin de Porres had a rough start in life. He lived in Lima, Peru, surrounded by rich and powerful people. Had things been just a little different, he could have been a part of that wealth too. But Martin's life took a different turn.

For you see, Martin de Porres's parents weren't married. His mother, Ana, was an African woman who had once been a slave but was now free. His father, Juan, was one of the conquistadors who had traveled to South America from Spain to make his fortune.

Juan had not made his fortune, but he was still a wealthy man of high position in Peru, where Martin was born. Not long afterward, another baby was born, Martin's sister. Not long after that, Juan left Peru and went to Ecuador, leaving Ana with little money and leaving the two children with no father.

Those were hard times, but Ana must have done a fine job, even by herself. As a child, little Martin was known around his neighborhood for being a very kind, generous boy.

When Martin was eight years old, his father returned and took him back to Ecuador. It was clear to everyone that Martin was intelligent, so his father hired a tutor to help his son learn to read and write. After two years, Juan took Martin back to his mother in Lima and told her to continue his education. Martin was to enter training to become a barber.

A barber?

You're probably wondering why Martin's father wanted him to be a barber and why it would take so much education for him to learn how to do the job.

Well, in those days, both in Europe and in South America, a barber did a lot more than just cut hair and trim the beards of the conquistadors.

Barbers were also doctors. Barbers bandaged wounds and set broken legs and arms. They knew all about the healing power of herbs and ointments, so they were really pharmacists too. Barbers even did simple kinds of surgery.

So as you can see, Martin was training for a very important job!

Martin enjoyed helping people, but soon he knew that being a barber in the middle of the city and living that busy kind of life was not really what he wanted. Martin wanted to keep helping, but he wanted to do it in a place where he could focus on God more. So

Martin joined a Dominican community. He never took vows as a brother or a priest, but he followed the Dominican way of life faithfully as a layperson.

Martin spent his entire life with those Dominicans, and it was a life full of love and generosity toward all of God's creatures. Martin was the person the other brothers went to when they were sick. No matter what, when the brothers fell ill, Martin was at their side with bandages, cool cloths, and ointments.

The poor people of the city also came to Martin for help, and he never turned anyone down, even when it made his superiors kind of angry.

You see, the place where the hundreds of Dominican brothers lived and worked was really and truly their home. They always did what they could to help others, but they also needed privacy so that they could pray and perform their daily tasks. But Martin just kept bringing sick strangers inside!

If there was a vacant room in the monastery, Martin didn't see any sense in letting it go to waste. It would be a perfect place for a poor, sick beggar to rest and get better for a while.

Martin didn't stay inside the monastery all the time. He spent a lot of his time in the city, helping the poor of Lima. Every day, Martin begged for alms on the streets of the city. He actually had a very strict system for what he did with the money he received. The money he received on Tuesdays and Wednesdays went to help a group of more than 160 poor families. The Thursday and Friday money went to poor students and priests. The Sunday coins were used for clothing and food for slaves and native peoples. And finally, the money he received on Saturdays and Mondays was donated to churches for masses for the souls in purgatory.

Martin was full of love and compassion, and it kept him very busy. But Martin still made time to care for yet one other group: animals.

St. Martin de Porres

Many saints are remembered for treating animals with care. That's because when your heart is filled with God's love, that love is for every part of God's creation. Saints hate to see any of God's creatures suffering at all.

Martin loved all kinds of animals, and many pictures of him show mice running around his feet. Here's why.

The brothers in Martin's monastery were going absolutely mad with frustration. Mice and rats were multiplying and doing terrible damage to everything. They were eating the food and had even started testing their tiny little teeth on the priests' vestments. Something had to be done!

So of course, the brothers set a trap, and soon one of the tiny criminals was caught inside.

Martin couldn't stand the thought of the mice being killed. As the story goes, he bent over, took the mouse in his hand, and whispered, "Go, little brother, and tell your friends not to do us any more harm. Come every day to the back of the garden, and I'll feed you."

The brothers were amazed to see the mouse and all of his friends follow Martin right out the door.

Another time, Martin saw the frightened little eyes of another mouse peeking out from behind a corner while a dog and a cat ate peacefully from the same dinner bowl. Martin brought the mouse over too and watched happily as the three former enemies shared a meal!

The whole city of Lima knew about Martin. They knew about his heart, which never tired of helping the poor and sick. They knew about his care of animals and his deep understanding of healing herbs and other plants. They knew about his soul, which was on fire for the love of God. When Martin was dying, the ruler of Peru came to his bedside and knelt beside him, asking for Martin's blessing.

Martin de Porres's life was certainly difficult at first. He could have spent his time wishing his life were different.

But he didn't. Martin had his gifts. He heard God's voice in his heart calling him to use them. So Martin obeyed, in love and joy. Just think of how many people he helped.

So don't waste your time wishing your life was different. The life God gave you is full of goodness just as it is. Don't wait around to use it. Take that big step right now!

St. Martin de Porres accepted his life as it was and used his time to help others. Are there parts of your life that you find hard to accept?

Blessed Joseph de Veuster *1840–1889*

May 10

Love is the most wonderful thing in the world, isn't it?

How do you know it's wonderful? Think about these things: A hug from your mom or dad. A big kiss from your little sister. A long talk with a good friend who understands.

All of these things come from loving hearts.

Love certainly is wonderful. It's also risky. And dangerous. And love, believe it or not, can hurt more than anything.

Think about how disappointed your parents are when you do something bad. If they didn't love you, they wouldn't be disappointed, because they wouldn't care about you or your actions.

Think about how bad you feel when your little sister is awake all night, sick with a fever and crying. You're sad, and not just because you're not getting any sleep either. You're sad because she's hurting and you can't do much to stop the hurt. If you didn't care—if you didn't love her—her cries wouldn't bother you in the same way.

Yes, loving is a happy choice. But it's also a risk. When we love, we're choosing to care. And when people we care about are hurting, we hurt too.

That's love. It's a choice we make every day. And for most of us, the little hurts that loving brings don't last very long.

Blessed Joseph de Veuster made a choice to love too. But his choice was more serious than anything most of us can imagine.

He chose to love, and he knew that his choice would bring him deep pain. In fact, he knew that the love he chose would bring him more than pain. It would bring him death.

Joseph de Veuster chose to love people who suffered from leprosy.

Nowadays, leprosy, or Hansen's disease, is curable. But it wasn't in the nineteenth century, when Joseph lived. Once a person was diagnosed with leprosy, he or she was sure to die within a few years. Joseph knew this, but he chose to love lepers anyway.

Joseph was born in Belgium. After he had completed his studies for the priesthood, he took the name Fr. Damien. Then he was chosen for a special mission. He was chosen to go to Hawaii.

In those days, Hawaii was not yet a part of the United States. It was an independent country called the Sandwich Islands. The islands were ruled by a king and a queen. Many foreigners lived there, including many Catholic priests and sisters who ran schools and helped the poor and the sick.

That's what Damien traveled across two oceans to do. He went across the Atlantic, down around the very tip of South America, then up again through the Pacific Ocean to Hawaii.

A few years after he arrived, Damien heard about a terrible situation on one of the islands. There were people with leprosy in Hawaii. The rulers of the islands were afraid that the leprosy would spread, so they set aside part of one island for the lepers. If you were discovered to have leprosy, you were put on a ship and sent to this island, called Molokai. You didn't have a choice.

Believe it or not, the rulers of Hawaii sent lepers to Molokai with not much more than the clothes on their backs. There were no doctors to help them. Ships dropped off supplies for the lepers, but only occasionally. The lepers lived in desperate poverty, with no one to help them as their sickness got worse.

Fr. Damien heard about the lepers on Molokai, and it didn't take him any time to decide what he would do. He would go and help them. Do you know what that meant for Fr. Damien?

Leprosy is spread through touch and through the air. When people have leprosy, their fingers, toes, and noses can be eaten away by the disease. It is a very painful and awful disease.

Fr. Damien knew all this. He knew that if he went to live with the lepers, he would die this way.

But he went anyway. The lepers needed help. They needed God's love to give them strength in their suffering and in their death. They needed to live in peace and dignity while they could.

If we hear about someone in need, and we can help, how can we say no?

When Fr. Damien arrived at the island, he found an awful sight. The lepers lived in filthy huts. They had no fresh water and little healthy food. Of course, they had no bandages for their wounds. They had nothing to take their minds off their misery except alcohol.

Fr. Damien went right to work. He was a strong man, full of energy and used to doing hard work. All by himself, he started building better homes for the lepers. He built a chapel and taught the lepers how to plant gardens for fresh food. He was so busy that for the first few weeks, he didn't even bother to build himself a home—he slept under the wide, spreading branches of a big tree!

Within months, the life of the lepers changed. They were still sick and Fr. Damien had to perform one funeral every day, but something important had happened. From the beginning,

Fr. Damien had been determined to love the lepers. He wouldn't be afraid, as other people were, to be close to them or touch them. He would share meals with them and befriend them. Through this love, Fr. Damien taught the lepers that they were God's children. He taught them that they had dignity and that they could live with dignity.

The lepers began to take pride in their settlement. Fr. Damien formed a choir that sang beautifully at masses. He taught them how to play all kinds of donated musical instruments. They painted the chapel in bright, bold colors. Fr. Damien convinced the government to send regular shipments of food and building supplies.

And every day, since there were no doctors or nurses at the settlement, Fr. Damien spent his mornings washing the lepers' sores and bandaging their wounds. If a patient needed to have part of his or her body amputated, Fr. Damien did that too.

So it's no wonder that one Sunday, after being on the island a few years, Fr. Damien began his homily in a new way. He said, slowly and carefully, so that everyone would understand, "We lepers . . ."

Fr. Damien was now one of them. He had leprosy.

He died four years later. He suffered the way anyone with leprosy suffered, and his body showed the same wounds. He worked until almost the very end of his life. When he could no longer leave his hut, his friends on the island would gather around the windows and doors of his hut, singing softly to him and giving him the same kind of comfort he had tried to give them for so many years.

Jesus loved and kept loving even though he knew it would bring his body suffering and pain. Fr. Damien loved this way too, freely and without thinking twice about it.

Blessed Joseph de Veuster helped others even though he knew that he would lose his life as a result of it. When you think about helping others, do you stop and count the cost, or do you just step up and help?

 PART 14

SAINTS ARE

People Who Help in Ordinary Ways

*The kingdom of heaven is like a
mustard seed that a person took and
sowed in a field. It is the smallest
of all the seeds, yet when full-grown
it is the largest of plants.*

Matthew 13:31–32

St. Christopher   *3rd century*

July 25

You're a special person.

Do you know why? You're special and unique because every single person is special and unique.

God made you, and he didn't make you by accident. He did it all on purpose when he gave you that red hair, that brain that can figure out hard math problems, those legs that can run really fast, and that smile that makes other people feel so happy.

Yes, God knew exactly what he was doing when he created you.

He knew that there would be jobs in this world that would have to get done and that only you would be able to do them. He knew that there would be people who needed help and that you would be the one to help them, because God made you strong and caring enough to help.

Sometimes, though, it might be hard to understand how God wants you to help. You have to try and try again. That's exactly what St. Christopher had to do.

St. Christopher is one of the most famous saints of all. You might have a St. Christopher medal, or your parents might have a little statue of St. Christopher in their car. Your name might even be Christopher!

We don't know much about Christopher. We do know that he was one of the many Christians killed by the Romans when

Christianity was new. He voluntarily died for his faith, so he was what we call a martyr. But the stories we tell most often about Christopher aren't about his death. They're the stories about his life that we've invented to help us figure out the best way to serve God.

It's said that Christopher was a very big man. He was almost a giant, in fact. He also had a big heart, and he told his friends and family that he wanted to use his strength to help the most powerful person in the world.

Who do you think that was? A king, perhaps? Christopher thought so. He traveled to the court of a powerful king and offered his services. The king gratefully accepted, for he had a lot of work that Christopher could do.

Christopher helped guard the king. He frightened off enemies. He lifted the king onto his huge, massive horse. Christopher was happy, because he thought he was serving the most powerful person in the world.

But over time, Christopher noticed something strange. The king seemed strong and powerful most of the time, but not always. Whenever someone mentioned one particular name, the king's face fell and he made a strange sign over himself, from his head to his chest and then to his shoulders.

What was that name? It was the devil's name—Satan.

Christopher asked the king why he made the strange sign. The king told him that the sign helped protect him against Satan's great power.

So it seemed to Christopher that the king wasn't the most powerful man in the world after all. Christopher decided to go find this Satan, who was supposedly even more powerful than a king.

On Christopher's journey, he met a man on the road, and he asked him where he might find Satan. Christopher didn't know it, but the man was Satan. When Christopher found this out, he offered to serve him, not knowing that Satan was responsible for all evil.

The devil gladly accepted Christopher's offer. He could use a big, strong helper.

The two started off down the road, but the devil saw something in the distance and began to shake with fear. As they drew closer to the spot, Christopher could tell that the devil was growing more and more afraid. What was it? All Christopher could see was two pieces of wood nailed together at the side of the road.

They finally reached the spot, and the devil could stand it no longer. He turned around and ran as fast as he could in the opposite direction.

Now that Christopher was close enough, he could see a carved figure on the wood. It was a man, his feet and hands nailed to the cross. Christopher stopped to think. The king had been less powerful than Satan, but Satan must be less powerful than this man on the cross. But who was this man?

In the next village, Christopher got his answer. The man on the cross was Jesus Christ, the Son of God.

"How can I serve him?" Christopher wanted to know.

No one could answer him, but they told him to go find an old man—a hermit—who lived in a cave outside the village.

Christopher found him and said, "I want to serve the most powerful person in the world. I understand that Jesus is that person. How can I serve him?"

The hermit told him that he must fast and pray to find Jesus. Christopher answered that he couldn't really do either. If he fasted, he would grow too weak to do his work. And he didn't know how to pray.

"Well then," the old hermit said, "there is a river at the bottom of the mountain that is very difficult to cross. You are big and strong. Why don't you go there and help travelers cross the river?"

That's what Christopher did. Every day and every night, he let weary and frightened travelers climb onto his strong back, and then he carried them across the river. When he put them down on the other side of the river, they could continue on to their warm homes.

One night, a child appeared. He was just a tiny boy, traveling all alone. It was raining, and the river was very rough. Of course the child needed help to cross. Christopher was ready.

He put the tiny boy on his back and started across the river. The rain came down, and the cold river water washed around Christopher's legs. It shouldn't have been hard to carry the boy across the river, since the boy was very small. But as Christopher made his way through the cold rain, he noticed that the boy was getting heavier. With every step, Christopher had to work harder, because he was getting so terribly weighed down. He was afraid that he might not even make it and the little boy would drown. By the time he got to the other side, Christopher could barely walk. He set the little boy down and brushed the water from his eyes.

"How are you so heavy?" he asked. "I felt as if I were carrying the weight of the world on my shoulders."

The little boy looked at Christopher. "You were," he answered, "and the one who made it."

Christopher had found Christ at last. And how had he found him? Once Christopher had learned about God, the most powerful one of all, he knew that the only way to live happily was to put God first. Thanks to the old hermit, Christopher had found that his way of serving God was special.

St. Christopher

St. Christopher served Jesus by helping others across a river. Can you think of simple things you can do to help make the lives of others around you easier?

St. Blaise *d. 316*

February 3

Feeling sick is the pits, isn't it?

Your nose is all stuffed up, you're coughing so much you can't even sleep, your stomach's upset all the time, and those little elves won't stop hammering on your head.

And then there's the sore throat. It hurts to swallow anything, and eating is almost a punishment.

Oh, it's terrible to feel sick. When you feel like that, what do you want people to do for you?

It would be nice if they could give you a magic pill that made all the pain go away instantly, but that miracle drug hasn't been invented yet. Meanwhile, isn't it nice when people—Mom, Dad, Grandma—take care of you in simple ways?

They bring you juice and soup. They help you get comfortable and tuck that extra blanket around you. They sit with you, talk to you, read you stories, and play games with you.

It doesn't make the sickness go away, but it sure makes you feel a little better, doesn't it?

Most saints spent a lot of time helping others in small ways. St. Blaise was such a saint.

We don't know a lot about St. Blaise, but what we do know tells us that people remembered him as a person who cared a lot about sick people. We know for sure that Blaise was a bishop. He was the bishop of a town in Armenia. He may have been a doctor too.

One story about Blaise goes this way. When the Roman rulers started persecuting Christians where Blaise lived, he escaped to a cave to hide. There in the wilderness, Blaise lived in a cold, dark, rocky cave. He wasn't alone, though. He had friends— wild animals!

It's said that this cave was where sick animals came to suffer and die. They were all there—wolves, bears, and even big wildcats.

But these animals never hurt Blaise. Why? Because he cared for them. He bandaged up their wounds and made medicines from the roots and berries he found. In these little ways, Blaise helped the wild animals feel better. In return, they never harmed him.

But one day, Blaise was discovered and arrested by the Romans. On the journey back to the town, they encountered a woman who was holding her little son and crying for help. The little boy was choking on a fishbone that was stuck in his throat.

In chains, on his way to certain death, Blaise asked the soldiers to stop. He prayed for strength, and with God's help, he removed the fishbone that was about to kill that little boy.

There's another story about Blaise's journey to prison. It's said that he saw a wolf running through a field with a squealing pig in its fierce jaws. A woman ran after them. She was a very poor woman, and she told Blaise that the wolf had stolen the pig, which was to be her only source of food over the cold winter months.

Blaise had lived with animals, and he understood them. He stopped the wolf, gently released the pig, and returned it to the woman. The poor woman was so grateful that when Blaise was in prison, she brought him food for nourishment and candles to light up the dark prison cell.

After spending some time in prison, Blaise was killed by the Romans. He was one of thousands of Christians killed during those terrible times, just because he had faith in Jesus. We remember and honor him for that.

But we also remember him for something simpler. St. Blaise brought comfort to people, and even animals, when they were sick and feeling bad.

If you've ever had your throat blessed on February 3, the feast day of St. Blaise, you might see how all this fits together. At Mass on this day, the priest takes two candles—like the candles the poor lady brought to Blaise in prison—and blesses your throat. He asks God to protect you from diseases of the throat and all other illnesses too. He makes an X with the two candles and puts them gently across your throat, just as Blaise laid his hands on the throat of the little boy who was choking.

His is a simple way to follow Jesus. It doesn't take much time or great sacrifice. But we all know how much that little bowl of soup or that cool hand on our forehead can help.

So when someone in your house is sick, it would be a good time to think of St. Blaise—and then do what you can to help. Giving sick people a bit of comfort—now that's a simple way of loving that even a kid can do.

St. Blaise served Jesus by comforting people who were sick. What are some simple ways you can help the sick and suffering in your family?

St. Anthony of Padua *1195–1231*

June 13

Following Jesus isn't just for Sundays or special occasions.

It's for every day. We don't have to follow all sorts of complicated rules to follow Jesus. We can follow him in many simple, ordinary ways.

Saints know this, of course. Even the saints who led extraordinary lives, who started hospitals and schools or died dramatic deaths as martyrs, know this. They know that we only have the strength to take great big steps toward God when we've been taking lots of little steps all along.

It's like writing poetry or dancing in a ballet or pitching a baseball. You can't write beautiful poems unless you learn the alphabet first. You can't dance the lead in a ballet unless you learn the five positions and all those little steps first. You can't pitch a baseball well without a lot of practice.

Following Jesus starts with little steps too. You tell the truth about that broken window, or you keep quiet when you're tempted to talk back to Dad. You watch television five minutes less than usual and spend some time with God instead.

These ordinary little steps help us see a very important truth: God's with us all the time, helping us make the right decisions, no matter how small they may seem. For you see, God doesn't just care about major catastrophes and big problems. He cares about the tiniest parts of our lives. That's what Jesus is saying when he reminds us that God takes care of the birds in the air and the flowers in the field, just as he takes care of us—in ordinary ways, day to day, hour to hour, and minute to minute.

Saints are a part of God's plan for caring too. Although they have died, they are still a part of our lives. We know that since they're with God in heaven, they can still help us. That's why we pray to saints. We're not worshiping them. We're just talking to them, asking them to pray for us.

It's pretty simple, really. We ask friends to pray for us and help us all the time. Saints are friends who happen to live in heaven instead of down the street. Can they still help us? Of course they can, and because they're filled with the same kind of love that God has, they want to help us take those small steps in faith that help make us stronger for the big challenges.

One of the most loved friends in heaven is St. Anthony of Padua. Your church might have a statue of him, and you might even have a holy card with his picture on it. People ask St. Anthony for help all the time, and for the most ordinary things, and that's okay. Like a good friend, St. Anthony is always willing to help. People especially like to ask St. Anthony to help them find things that are lost. In a minute, we'll find out why.

We turn to St. Anthony for help with our ordinary problems, but his life was really anything but ordinary. St. Anthony was born in Portugal, and when he grew up, he studied to be a priest. He was a brilliant student and knew the Bible backward and forward. Someone once said that if all the Bibles in Europe were burned, it wouldn't be a terrible problem. People could just go to St. Anthony, and he could write the Scriptures down for them!

Anthony was a good teacher, but one day something happened that inspired him to follow Jesus in a slightly different way. Five Franciscan priests had traveled to Morocco, a country in Africa, to preach the good news about Jesus. They were brutally killed, and what was left of their bodies was brought to the town where Anthony lived.

Anthony couldn't sit still any longer. More than anything, he wanted to go to Morocco himself and try to give the love of Jesus to the people who had done this terrible thing. No one seemed to need Christ's love more than people who would torture and kill innocent men.

So Anthony joined the Franciscan order, got on a ship, and sailed to Morocco. Things didn't work out as he had hoped, though. He fell ill soon after he arrived and had no choice but to return to Europe.

Anthony's plans weren't working out, but perhaps that's because God had something else in mind for him. The ship Anthony was on, the one he thought was taking him back to university life in Portugal, got blown off course by a sudden strong wind. It went straight to the island of Sicily, where a huge meeting of Franciscan brothers happened to be taking place at that very moment.

Anthony didn't speak at the meeting, since he was really an outsider. He sat silently and listened. Perhaps he even heard St. Francis of Assisi speaking of holy poverty as the way to follow Jesus and of how important it is to preach the love of Jesus to all people, especially the poor.

After the meeting, Anthony continued to live a quiet life as a friar, working in a hospital in Italy, taking the humblest jobs of all. Back in Portugal, Anthony had already begun to gain fame as a scholar and teacher, but he said not a word about that in the hospital. He worked hard in the kitchen and the garden, helping the sick in the most ordinary, everyday ways.

Then one day something happened that was almost as strange as the ship wandering off course. There was a large meeting of Franciscans and Dominicans, but oddly enough, the plans for who would give the sermon at the meeting fell through. There were plenty of fine preachers present, but none of them were prepared.

Those in charge of the meeting went down the line of friars. "Would you care to give the sermon, Brother? No? What about you, Father? No? Well, what about you, Fr. Anthony—is that your name?"

Slowly, Anthony rose, and just as slowly, he began to speak. The other friars sat up to listen. There was something very special about Anthony. He didn't use complicated language, but his holiness and love for God shone through his words. He was one of the best preachers they had ever heard!

From that point on, Anthony's quiet life in the hospital kitchen was over. For the rest of his life, he traveled around Italy and France, preaching sermons in churches and town squares to people who came from miles around.

His listeners heard Anthony speak about how important it is for us to live every day in God's presence. As a result of his words, hundreds of people changed their lives and bad habits, bringing Jesus back into their hearts.

Anthony wasn't always successful, though. In most cities, businesspeople would shut down their shops to come listen to Anthony. But in one city the townspeople closed their hearts to him and listened with hard faces and harsh eyes.

St. Anthony had done his best. He shrugged and turned around. The fish in the bay poked their heads out of the water to see what was going on, and St. Anthony started preaching to them instead!

Now, back to the first question. Why do we ask St. Anthony to help us find lost things?

St. Anthony had a book of psalms that was quite special to him. It was special because in those days before the printing press, books were rare and expensive. But it was also special because it contained many notes Anthony had made to help him in his preaching and teaching.

St. Anthony of Padua

Late one night, a young Franciscan decided to leave the community. He'd had enough of that life, so he made plans to just sneak out in the middle of the night. He saw Anthony's book of psalms on his way out, and he snatched it up and ran. He knew that he could sell this precious book for a good deal of money.

Of course, Anthony was quite upset. He prayed that God would change the young man's heart and bring him back to the Franciscan life. He also hoped that while God was at it, he would return Anthony's book too.

The next day, the young man returned, tired and ashamed, with Anthony's book. He also brought back his own gifts and talents, which he decided once more to offer to the Franciscan community.

So that's why we like to ask St. Anthony to help us find lost things. He was an extraordinary man who can still help us from heaven, even in the most ordinary ways.

St. Anthony of Padua was willing to use his extraordinary, God-given gifts to help others take small steps towards Jesus. What small steps toward or away from Jesus have you taken today?

St. Bernard of Montjoux *c. 996–c. 1081*

May 28

Traveling is usually pretty fun, isn't it?

There are so many interesting things to see no matter where you go: big, exciting cities, the mountains, the sea, little towns full of history.

But sometimes, things can go wrong.

Maybe it's happened to your family. A tire goes flat or the engine overheats. Someone gets sick and needs help right away. Or all the motels are full, it's late at night, and you just don't know what you're going to do!

Those are miserable times, and they can ruin a whole trip. So isn't it wonderful when, out of the blue, someone steps in to help?

Another driver stops to help you change that tire or to drive your dad to the gas-station. A helpful person in a store calls a doctor for you. Just when you think your family will never find a place to spend the night, a gas-station attendant tells you that there's a motel just a few miles down the road. What a relief! And what a blessing all those nice people are!

Well, believe it or not, helping travelers has always been an important part of Christian life. Long before hotels or motels, monasteries especially were known as places where tired travelers could find some warmth and a bite to eat, with no questions asked.

St. Bernard of Montjoux

Why has it been an important part of Christian life? Because from the very beginnings of his life, Jesus was a traveler. He was born away from home. When he grew up, he spent his days and nights walking up, down, and around the land of Palestine, teaching, healing, and forgiving.

So when Jesus spoke of all the ways we're called to help each other, one of the things he said was "When I was a stranger, you welcomed me." Whenever we offer a smile, food, drink, and shelter to a stranger, we're reaching out to Jesus, who is living in that person.

St. Bernard was a monk who lived long ago. We remember him today for the help he offered travelers.

St. Bernard lived high in the Alps, the tall mountain range that divides Italy from the western part of Europe. He was a bishop in charge of many villages scattered throughout those mountains. He did much good work, helping start churches and schools in those lands that hugged the sky.

But something bothered Bernard. A lot of people needed help but weren't getting it. These people were travelers.

People liked to travel in those days, even though there were no cars, airplanes, or trains. They traveled for their business. They traveled to go to war. They traveled to find better jobs. And many people traveled to Italy to go pray in Rome, the center of the Christian church.

The problem was that to get into Italy from much of the rest of Europe, travelers had to cross the Alps. They had to climb on foot or push their tired donkeys and horses up, up, up those enormous mountains. They had to follow narrow, dangerous paths that were often covered with snow. Travelers got lost all the time. They fell down steep hills. They got weak and sick and sometimes froze to death. Robbers hid around corners and behind rocks, waiting to rob travelers, whose cries for help would be heard by no one in those lonely mountain regions. It was an extremely difficult journey.

There was one divide in the mountains where it was a little easier to cross, so the road there was busy. Bernard decided that this would be the perfect spot to set up a place to help travelers. It was eight thousand feet above sea level.

He called it a "hospice," but it was a lot like what you'd call a hotel—without room service, of course. Bernard and his fellow monks built the hospice themselves. They welcomed all travelers at any time of day, no matter what country they came from or what their religion was. They provided warm food and extra clothes. They comforted exhausted travelers by giving them a roof over their heads.

And every morning, the monks set out through the snow. In their robes, with lanterns and walking sticks, the monks searched. They searched for the injured, the lost, and the half-frozen. Everyone they found was rushed back to the hospice.

St. Bernard did all he could to offer help to travelers. But we also remember him for another reason. Have you ever heard of the dogs called Saint Bernards? You might be wondering what they had to do with St. Bernard.

Those dogs were indeed first bred in the Alps. We don't know if St. Bernard himself used the dogs, but by the nineteenth century, the monks in his hospice certainly did. The huge, furry, faithful dogs helped the monks find lost travelers. They even brought the travelers a bit of water in those little barrels they wore around their necks.

Just like St. Bernard, they helped travelers too!

St. Bernard and his monks followed Jesus by giving travelers food, shelter, and a place to rest. People travel through our lives all the time, and some of them even need help. What are some things we can do to help ourselves see when someone traveling through our lives could use help?

PART 15

People Who Come from All Over the World

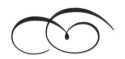

Go, therefore, and make disciples of all nations, baptizing them in the name of the Father, and of the Son, and of the holy Spirit.

Matthew 28:19

Blessed Kateri Tekakwitha *1656–1680*

July 14

Have you ever met
someone who helped
you see life in a new
way?

Maybe you've experienced something that's made everything
seem different. Hard experiences, such as being in an accident or
having someone you know die, can do that to you. Good experiences
can make a big difference too, but in a different way. Maybe you
have a teacher who believes in you and who makes learning fun.
Or maybe you travel to some new place, one that changes your life.

Whatever it is, that experience helped you see things in a new,
better way. You might say that it helped you see what was really
important in life and what should come first.

A long time ago, in the most northern part of what we now call
New York State, a young Mohawk girl met some strangers who
helped her understand what was most important in her life, in ways
that were quite surprising.

When she was born, her parents named her Tekakwitha, which,
like all Native American names, has a meaning. The baby's name
meant "she puts things in order."

Life was difficult for the baby's family and tribe. They had to
work hard for food and shelter. The winters were terribly cold, and
sometimes the tribes went to war with each other.

There were other troubles too. For many years, the Mohawks had
been visited now and then by men from across the vast Atlantic Ocean.

These men, some French, some English, brought strange new things with them. Some of the things were good, but some were quite bad.

One of those bad things was a sickness called smallpox. Thanks to modern medicine, people don't get smallpox anymore. But back then, it was an awful disease. It was like chicken pox, only worse. The spots were bigger and went deeper into your skin. Many people died from smallpox.

The French, English, and Spanish people who came to America in those early days brought smallpox with them without even knowing it. Smallpox killed many Native Americans in those years.

The sickness came to Tekakwitha's village. When she was four years old, her parents died of smallpox, and she caught it too. She didn't die, but it gave her terrible scars and harmed her eyes.

What a sad time. Smallpox left Tekakwitha with no parents, scars all over her face, and poor eyesight. Luckily, the little girl was taken care of by an uncle. As she grew older and was able to work more, she was a great help to him.

Then one day, Tekakwitha's life changed forever, thanks to a visit by two strangers.

The strangers were Frenchmen, and this time, instead of bringing bad things, they brought something wonderful: the good news of Jesus.

The Native Americans called the strangers "Black Robes" because that is what they wore: long, black robes and big, black flat hats. They were priests (like Saint Isaac Jogues) who had traveled across the sea to teach the Native Americans about the love of Jesus.

Tekakwitha was twelve years old when the Black Robes came to her village. She listened carefully to what they said about the great Spirit who had come to earth and who had become a man named

Jesus. She heard them talk about the great peace that comes into our hearts when we believe in Jesus and follow his way of love.

Right away, Tekakwitha knew that what they were saying was true. She wanted to be baptized.

But there was a problem. She still lived with her uncle, and if she became a Christian, it would bother him a lot. So for eight years, she waited. She kept working hard, helping her uncle, and listening to the priests, learning more and more about Jesus.

When Tekakwitha was twenty years old, she could wait no longer. She asked to be baptized, and she was. She was given the Christian name Catherine, which translates into her language as "Kateri." She was also known as the "Lily of the Mohawks."

Kateri's heart was at peace. But soon, trouble began.

Her family and neighbors wanted her to marry. They mocked her for her beliefs. No one else among them had become a Christian. Kateri asked if she could not work on Sundays, in order to keep that as her day of worship. Her family agreed, but they said that if she didn't work that day, she wouldn't eat either.

Even with the opposition from her Native American community, Kateri stayed close to God. She prayed the rosary and depended on God to help her stay strong.

Just think how hard it would be to be the only person in your family or school who was a Christian. Just imagine how it would feel if every day people made fun of your beliefs and tried to get you to change. You can see how strong Kateri had to be.

After some time, Kateri heard about a village many miles away that the Black Robes had built especially for Christian Native Americans. The priests knew how hard it was for them to be all alone in their faith, so they made a place in what we now call Canada where Christians could live, work, and pray together in peace.

Kateri decided to move there, and late one night, without anyone knowing, she left.

After a long journey over land and up the river, Kateri reached the village, which was called a "prayer fort." It was a wonderful place where she could work hard, be with friends, and pray all she wanted without anyone making fun of her. The other villagers told stories about Kateri's deep love for God and her kindness in caring for the sick. They said that she arrived at the chapel door at four every morning and waited for it to open. People learned how wonderful God's love was just by watching Kateri pray, because her face was filled with such deep peace and joy.

We can be happy that Kateri was able to reach the prayer fort and live among friends, because just a year or so after she arrived, she grew critically ill and died. She was twenty-four years old.

Do you remember what *Tekakwitha* means? It means "she puts things in order."

That's just what Blessed Kateri Tekakwitha did, isn't it? All alone, with no one to encourage or support her, she put God first, and while she lived, she nourished a peaceful, loving heart. It's that simple witness to God's love that led the church to name her "Blessed"—the first Native American to be so honored.

Don't you wonder what the world would be like if everyone put God first? You can be sure that it would be a much different place.

I wonder who's brave enough to start . . .

Blessed Kateri Tekakwitha knew what was most important in her life. If you had to list what was most important in your life, what would come first?

St. Paul Miki and Companions *d. 1597*

February 6

Sometimes when we think of what our faith is all about, we think pretty small.

We think that our faith isn't about much more than our own family prayers, our own parish, and our own town. We forget that God's love is for every bit of creation and that all over the world, boys and girls of different colors and cultures share something really important with us: our faith in Jesus.

As we've seen in our other saints' stories, it took many years and almost unbelievable sacrifice for the good news of Jesus to reach every corner of the world. It was slow because people couldn't travel as quickly as we can now. Up until the 1800s (when trains and engines were invented), travelers made their trips in many ways. Some had to walk. Some rode on horses or donkeys, and some were pulled in carriages. Others crossed the sea in boats that were powered by sails or by other human beings who were chained below deck and forced to row with enormous long oars.

So getting that good news to every corner of the earth took a long time.

For example, Japan didn't hear the good news until the 1500s, when St. Francis Xavier arrived on the shores of that great island nation. At first, the people and even the rulers of Japan were interested in Christianity. As St. Francis Xavier discovered, the Japanese were quite intelligent, and they enjoyed discussing religion and philosophy. Many Japanese people even welcomed Christianity, and it's said that within forty years of St. Francis Xavier's visit, more than two hundred thousand Japanese had embraced Christianity.

All was going well, it seemed. Japanese Christians lived peacefully, worshiping God, teaching their children, and helping the poor. But that peace wouldn't last. In fact, it was going to end in quite a terrible way, forcing Christianity to disappear from Japan for almost three hundred years.

It all started with a rumor. You know how harmful rumors can be.

The rumor spread and reached the rulers of Japan. It was whispered that Christianity was nothing more than a way for the Spanish and Portuguese rulers and merchants to come to Japan and eventually conquer it.

The Japanese rulers would have none of that. They immediately made it a crime to be a Christian.

What followed was a terrible time of persecution for Japanese Christians. For almost forty years, the Japanese rulers chased, arrested, tortured, and killed followers of Jesus' law of love. They treated the Christians in the most horrible ways so that all Japanese people would know that they could never listen to Christian preachers again.

Paul Miki was one of several Christians killed in the year 1597. These people came from all walks of life. There was a soldier and a doctor. One of the persecuted was a former pagan priest. Several children were arrested and tortured as well.

Paul Miki was the son of a noble and respected Japanese family. He was well educated in his faith, and he worked hard as a teacher of the faith. When Paul Miki was arrested, he was thirty-three years old.

His captors cut off part of his ear, just as they had with the other prisoners. The captors then chained the prisoners together and marched them through villages, letting the people see what would happen to them if they chose to follow Jesus.

St. Paul Miki and Companions

When the prisoners reached the place of execution, they were allowed to go to confession one last time. Then iron collars were clamped around their necks and chains were placed around their legs and arms. The prisoners were hung on crosses by these chains.

One soldier stood by each crucified prisoner, holding a raised sword. At the call from their leader, each soldier was to thrust his sword into the body of the prisoner in front of him. But before that moment, Paul Miki had a chance to speak.

Hanging from the cross, with iron chains around his neck, arms, and legs, his face bloody and his body beaten and weak, Paul Miki used his last moments on earth to help others.

He told those gathered there that following Jesus didn't make him a bad Japanese person. And, like Jesus, Paul Miki forgave those who had made him suffer and who were about to kill him.

"Ask Christ to help you become happy," he said. "I obey Christ. After Christ's example, I forgive my persecutors. I do not hate them. I ask God to have pity on all, and I hope my blood will fall on my fellow men as a fruitful rain."

The blood of Paul Miki and of the hundreds of Japanese Christians who were martyred did bear fruit. In the 1860s, the rulers of Japan once again opened their shores to foreigners, even foreign missionaries. Those missionaries found a very surprising thing: Catholics.

Japanese Catholics had worshiped in secret for three hundred years. They had not had good teachers, and some of their beliefs had strayed a bit, but after all those years, the faith and courage of Paul Miki and his companions hadn't been forgotten.

In one more corner of the world, the light of the good news had continued to flicker through the darkness, despite all the efforts to put it out for good.

That must be a very strong light, don't you think?

St. Paul Miki's faith put him into conflict with his government. Can you think of ways in which faith in Jesus might lead a person living in your time to disagree with certain aspects of life in his or her country?

Blessed Peter To Rot *1912–1945*

Peter To Rot was a Catholic his entire life.

His father, a tribal chief in Papua New Guinea (an island nation north of Australia), was the first on his island to invite Catholic missionaries to serve his people. So Peter was baptized as a baby and grew up in a faithful Catholic home.

As he grew up, Peter never stopped being interested in his faith. In fact, he was so interested in it that he was trained to be a teacher of the faith.

Peter was actually more than just a teacher. He was a lay catechist. Peter's family and friends had suggested that Peter study for this special job of lay catechist when he was eighteen. They had noticed how close he was to Jesus and how much he loved to help others.

A lay catechist is an assistant to missionary priests. There are many islands in Papua New Guinea, and they're very spread out. Even on the islands, villages were separated by rough roads that cut through jungles and mountains.

Missionaries couldn't be everywhere at once. They needed helpers to stay in the villages and help the new Catholics stay strong in their faith, even without a priest.

That's what Peter To Rot did. He went to school for two years to study, and when he returned, he was his village's lay catechist. He taught classes for children and grown-ups. He helped people with their problems. He prayed with people.

And when the priest could not be in the village for a long time, Peter baptized babies and anyone else who wanted to become Catholic. He led communion services.

Peter was happy in his job. Then, in 1936, he had another reason to be happy. He married a woman named Paula, and in a few years, he and his wife had three beautiful children.

But in 1942, life changed for Peter and for everyone else on the island. The Japanese, who were fighting in World War II, took over Papua New Guinea.

At first, the Japanese allowed life to continue as normal for the people. But as the war became more difficult, the Japanese started treating the villagers more harshly. First, they imprisoned all the foreign missionaries.

This meant that Peter and the other lay catechists had to serve their people all by themselves. They alone had the job of teaching and helping the people stay strong in their faith. Peter continued his work. He baptized people and led communion services. He even served at marriages and funerals.

The Japanese were concerned. They wanted more power over the people on the islands. So they decided to win the support of tribal chiefs who weren't Christian. The Japanese told the people that they should go back to practicing polygamy. This is marriage between a man and more than one wife.

Now, from the time Christians had come to Papua New Guinea, they had taught that polygamy was wrong. They could see that women in such marriages were treated badly. Peter continued to teach that polygamy was wrong, despite the efforts of the Japanese. He wouldn't agree to support it. He criticized it very openly.

So Peter was arrested by the Japanese.

Peter To Rot had been a faithful, joyful Catholic for all of his thirty-three years. There was no way he was going to give up his faith now, even though the Japanese soldiers who had imprisoned him were threatening to kill him if he didn't give in.

God had been faithful to Peter for Peter's whole life. Of course Peter would stay faithful to God.

Peter was held prisoner for two months. His prison was really a cave. During that time he was questioned over and over again and given chances to win his freedom by denying his faith.

Peter refused. He knew what was true. He knew what kind of world it would be if no one stood up for what was true.

Peter was allowed to have visitors, and when his mother came to visit one day, Peter told her that a doctor was coming to see him the next day. The doctor was bringing medicine, but Peter believed it wasn't really medicine.

He was right.

Peter was led into a room with the doctor. The doctor gave him a shot, then something to drink. In a few minutes, Peter started having terrible convulsions, and not long after that, he died.

The doctor had given Peter not medicine but poison.

Unafraid of the Japanese, hundreds of villagers from all around gathered for Peter's funeral. They couldn't say their prayers aloud in front of the soldiers, but the prayers in their hearts were strong.

They prayed in thanksgiving for the life of Peter To Rot. He had taught them about their faith. He had cared for them, prayed with them, baptized their babies, married them, and prayed over their dead. Peter had loved his own wife and children and had shown villagers from all around what a beautiful Christian marriage was like. And now Peter had been killed for believing in all these true things.

The people of Papua New Guinea never forgot Peter's witness to truth and love. When Pope John Paul II declared him Blessed in 1995, they had even more to celebrate. All the world would now know about the strength and courage Jesus gives his friends in every corner of the globe.

Blessed Peter To Rot didn't have to give his life for Jesus, but he did. What are some good things that you don't have to do but you choose to do anyway?

Blessed Maria Clementine Anuarite Nengapeta *1939–1964*

December 1

There are many different kinds of good news.

We get good news about family visits. We get good news about grades. We get good news about our health.

What would be the best news of all? What would be the most wonderful news you could ever hear?

How about this: God loves you. God made you on purpose, for a very special reason. God is with you every second of the day. God forgives your sins and gives you the strength to start over. God gave you a whole big world full of brothers and sisters. God came to earth as a man named Jesus.

Isn't it hard to sit still after hearing such wonderful news? Isn't it hard to keep it to yourself?

In story after story throughout this book, you've seen that saints are people who just can't keep quiet about that good news. They have to tell everyone.

They have to tell the poor. They have to tell powerful kings. They have to tell their family and friends. They have to tell their neighbors.

That's why so many of our saints are travelers. They take that good news to every corner of the earth. Think about it—a world full of millions of Christians started with just twelve apostles gathered in a room in a city called Jerusalem.

So anywhere you go on earth you'll find Christians. You'll find Christians in Europe and the Middle East. You'll find Christians in the Far East, Australia, and India. You'll find Christians from the tip of South America to the North Pole. And you'll find Christians in Africa.

Actually, Christianity came to Africa almost right after Jesus' resurrection. Some of the earliest and strongest Christian communities were in Egypt and Ethiopia, and there were others in the rest of northern Africa. Unfortunately, many of those Christian communities were simply wiped out by Muslim invaders in the early part of the eighth century. Only in the last two hundred years has Christianity started to grow in Africa once again.

And it really has grown. Many people say that in a few decades, most Christians in the world will be from Asia and Africa. That's quite a change, isn't it?

Africa has produced its fair share of saints, starting in ancient times with people like St. Monica and St. Augustine. But there are modern African saints too. Blessed Maria Clementine Anuarite Nengapeta is one.

Blessed Maria was born in a country called the Republic of the Congo. Her family wasn't Christian, but when she was four years old, Maria was baptized a Catholic Christian along with her mother and one of her sisters.

As she grew older, Maria felt a tug on her heart. She soon understood that the tug was from God, asking her to give her life to him. When she was fifteen, Maria said yes to God and joined a religious order so she could become a sister.

Maria's country was experiencing serious troubles during her life, but she continued to serve wherever she was needed. One day, Maria and some other sisters were traveling through the country when they were stopped by a soldier.

He gave all of the sisters a hard time for a little while, and then he focused his eyes on Maria. He prodded her side with his gun. He pushed her. And then the soldier threatened Maria. He tried to touch her in bad ways. Maria knew that this went against her vow to God. The soldier threatened her, saying that if she would not violate her vow, he would hurt her. He told her that nothing she'd said to God mattered anyway.

Maria refused. She'd made a promise to God, and she was going to keep it. For Maria, saying yes to the soldier would have been turning her back on God. She just wouldn't do it.

So the soldier shot Maria, killing her almost instantly.

It wasn't long before the news of Sister Maria's death spread throughout the country. Her fellow Christians grieved her death, but they thanked God for her strength too. Blessed Maria's strength came from exactly the same place as that of all the other saints we've met in this book.

When you have a best friend, you can't turn your back on her. If you betray that friend because you want to be more comfortable or safer, you'll probably end up being quite unhappy with yourself. You won't be comfortable at all. If you betray your friend because you are afraid of other people's opinions, you'll probably end up feeling bad about yourself, and that's worse than other people looking down on you.

The saints are best friends with God. We see this time and time again. They wouldn't betray God—not for money, not for comfort, not for family, and not even for safety.

They came from all over the world. They lived in every period of history. They had all kinds of unique gifts and talents.

But what makes them saints is that one special thing they all had in common. They all lived to share the news that God is waiting, with his arms outstretched, to be our best friend forever too.

Blessed Maria Clementine Anuarite Nengapeta, like all the saints, was best friends with God. What does it mean to have God as your best friend?

INDEX

Molla, Blessed Gianna Beretta, *14–16*

Monica, St., *19–22, 174, 302*

Monfort, St. Louis de, *89–92*

More, St. Thomas, *163–66*

Morone, Peter di. *See* St. Celestine V

N

Nazi party. *See* Nazis

Nazis, *168–69, 194, 245–47*

Nengapeta, Blessed Maria Clementine Anuarite, *301–4*

Neumann, St. John, *148–51*

Nicholas, St., *3–5*

O

Ozanam, Amélie, *35*

Ozanam, Blessed Frédéric, *32–36*

Ozanam, Marie, *35*

P

Padre Pio, Blessed, *108–12*

Patrick, St., *181–85*

Paul, St. Vincent de, *35, 255–59*

Perpetua, St., *225–28*

Peter To Rot, Blessed, *297–300*

Polycarp, St., *155–58*

Porres, St. Martin de, *260–64*

Pro, Humberto, *72*

Pro, Blessed Miguel, *69–73*

S

Sales, St. Francis de, *8*

Salesians, *8*

Seton, St. Elizabeth Ann, *9–13*

Seton, William, *9*

Simeon Stylites, St., *39–42*

Sisters of Charity, *12*

Sisters of the Blessed Sacrament, *221–22*

Solano, St. Francis, *127–30*

Soubirous, St. Bernadette, *104–7*

Stein, St. Edith, *191–94*

Stephen, St., *145*

T

Tekakwitha, Blessed Kateri, *289–92*

Teresa Benedicta of the Cross. *See* St. Edith Stein

Teresa of Ávila, St., *66–68, 85–88, 167, 193*

Theodosius (Roman emperor), *199–200*

Thérèse of Lisieux, St., *viii, 27–31*

Thor (god), *117–18*

V

Vandals, *142, 143*

Veuster, Blessed Joseph de, *265–68*

Vicchio, Guido da. *See* Blessed Fra Angelico

W

Wenceslaus, St., *145–47, 188*

X

Xavier, St. Francis, *123–26, 293–94*